Peter Bilhorn

Bilhorn's Male Chorus

Number 1

Peter Bilhorn

Bilhorn's Male Chorus
Number 1

ISBN/EAN: 9783337334628

Printed in Europe, USA, Canada, Australia, Japan

Cover: Foto ©Thomas Meinert / pixelio.de

More available books at **www.hansebooks.com**

Columbian Issue.

·1893·

❖

Bilhorn's Male Chorus

No. 1.

BY

PETER BILHORN.

ASSISTED BY E. M. HERNDON.

POCKET EDITION.

PUBLISHED BY

BILHORN BROS.,

Garden City Block, Rooms 716—717.
Randolph & Fifth Ave. CHICAGO, ILL.

PREFACE.

Because of the demand for a book of this kind
I have, by much prayer and thought, arranged the
Little "Pocket Edition" for young men, so they can
Have it with them at all times,
On all occasions, and in all places.
Remember Psalm xcvi., 1: O, sing unto the Lord a
New song.   Also, Psalm xxx., 4:
Sing unto the Lord, O ye saints of His.

Male choruses are growing to be
A needed feature to which young men
Long since ought to have been
Educated.

Christian young men should
Honor the Lord with their voices, and
Ought always to be
Ready to sing
Unto the Lord
Songs of redeeming love.

Yours for such,

Peter Bilhorn.

BILHORN'S MALE CHORUS.

POCKET EDITION.

No. 1.　　　　　　**Rouse, Ye Saints.**

C. H. Yatman.　　　　　　　　　　　　　　　　　　P. Bilhorn.

1. Rouse, ye saints, the world is dy-ing, We must work while it is day;
2. Wake, ye men, let us be do-ing, While the sun is in the sky;
3. Je - sus, Sav - ior, help our Spir-its, That we nev - er wea - ry be,

Sin-ners lost to us are cry-ing For the strait and nar-row way.
Let us seek the weak and err-ing, Precious souls that soon may die.
Lead-ing sin - ners to the Fountain Ev - er flow - ing full and free.

CHORUS

We will work from morn till night, By the Spir - it's pow'r and might,

Lead-ing men un - to the Light, Bless - ed Light of day!

No. 2.   Am I a Soldier.

Isaac Watts.   Thos. A. Arne. Cho. by P. B.

1. Am I a sol-dier of the cross— A foll-'wer of the Lamb,
2. Must I be car-ried to the skies On flow-'ry beds of ease:
3. Are there no foes for me to face? Must I not stem the flood?
4. Since I must fight if I would reign, In-crease my cour-age, Lord,

And shall I fear to own His cause, Or blush to speak His name?
While oth-ers fought to win the prize, And sailed thro' bloody seas?
Is this vile world a friend to grace, To help me on to God?
I'll bear the toil, en-dure the pain, Sup-port-ed by Thy word.

CHORUS.

Hal-le-lu - - jah! Hal-le-lu - - jah! Prais-es
Hal - le - lu - jah!   Hal-le - lu - jah!

to His ev-erlasting name we'll sing, Hal-le-lu - - jah! Hal-le-
Hal-le - lu-jah!

lu - - jah! We shall conquer thro' our Lord and King.
Hal - le - lu - jah!

No. 3.

Nearer Home To-day.

Arr.

P. Bilhorn.

Moderato.

1. One sweet-ly sol-emn tho't Comes to me o'er and o'er;
2. Near-er my Fa-ther's house, Where ma-ny man-sions be;
3. Near-er the bound of life Where bur-dens are laid down:
4. Be near me when my feet Are slip-ping o'er the brink;

Cres. *ff* *Rit.*

I'm near-er my Father's house to-day Than I have been be-fore.
I'm near-er the great white throne to-day, Yes, near to the crys-tal sea.
I'm near-er to leave the cross to-day, And near to re-ceive the crown.
I'm near-er my heav'nly home to-day, Per-haps than now I think.

CHORUS.

Near - er my home,..... Near - - er my home,........
Nearer my home, nearer my home, Nearer my beau-ti-ful, beau-ti-ful home,

p *ff* *p* *Rit.*

Near - - - er my home........ Than I have been be - fore.
Near-er my home, beau-ti-ful home, Than I have been be - fore.

No. 4. Where will You be?

Miss Ada Blenkhorn.

E. M. Herndon.

Con espressione.

1. Where will you be when life is o'er? When you have reached the
far - ther shore, Will Je - sus then your pi - lot be?
Will He then bid you "Fol - low me,"

2. No loved one can for you a - tone, You must be - fore Him
stand a - lone; At home with Christ then will you be?
Or where His face you can not see?

3. O pon - der well this ques - tion deep, Nor give your-self a-
gain to sleep, Un - til the Lord your por - tion be
For time and for e - ter - ni - ty.

4. If here your soul in Him doth live, E - ter - nal life to
you He'll give; To heav - en He will guide your way,
And o - pen wide the gates of day.

REFRAIN.

Where will you be, where will you be When you have crossed Death's sol - emn sea?

No. 5. Praises to Our King.

Miss Ada Blenkhorn.

P. Bilhorn.

1. We are chil-dren of the King, And our love and trib-ute bring,
2. Je-sus is our guard and guide, In His love we will con-fide,
3. Je-sus is a faith-ful friend, In His strength we may de-pend;

While His wor-thy praise we sing, And His grace pro-claim;
Keep-ing close to His dear side, That we may not stray;
He will keep us to the end, Trust-ing in His love.

He redeemed us with His blood, Washed us in His cleansing flood,
We will watch, and work and pray, In His footsteps walk al-way,
If the cross we dai-ly bear, We at last a crown shall wear,

Made us heirs and sons of God; Praise His ho-ly name.
Keep-ing in the nar-row way, Near His cross each day.
And His won-drous glo-ry share, In our home a-bove.

No. 6. Where Will You Spend Eternity?

Rev. E. A. Hoffman.

J. H. Tenney.

1. Where will you spend e - ter - ni - ty? That ques-tion comes to
2. Ma - ny are choos-ing Christ to - day, Turn - ing from all their
3. Leav - ing the strait and nar - row way, Go - ing the down-ward
4. Re - pent, be-lieve, this ver - y hour, Trust in the Sav - ior's

you and me! Tell me, what shall your an - swer be?
sins a - way; Heav'n shall their hap - py por - tion be:
road to - day, Sad will their fi - nal end - ing be,—
grace and pow'r, Then will your joy - ous an - swer be,

REFRAIN.

Where will you spend e - ter - ni - ty? E - ter - ni - ty!
Where will you spend e - ter - ni - ty? E - ter - ni - ty!
Lost thro' a long e - ter - ni - ty! E - ter - ni - ty!
Saved thro' a long e - ter - ni - ty! E - ter - ni - ty!

e - ter - ni - ty! Where will you spend e - ter - ni - ty?
e - ter - ni - ty! Where will you spend e - ter - ni - ty?
e - ter - ni - ty! Lost thro' a long e - ter - ni - ty!
e - ter - ni - ty! Saved thro' a long e - ter - ni - ty!

No. 7.   ## Jesus, Lover of My Soul.

P. Bilhorn.

1. Je - sus, lov - er   of   my   soul, Let me to Thy bo - som   fly,
2. Oth - er ref - uge have I   none, Hangs my help-less soul on   Thee;
3. Plenteous grace with Thee is found, Grace to cov - er   all my   sin;

While the near - er   wa - ters   roll, While the tem-pest still is   high;
Leave, ah, leave me   not a - lone, Still   sup-port and com-fort me.
Let   the heal-ing streams a - bound, Make and keep me pure with-in.

Cres.

Hide me, O   my Sav - ior, hide, Till the storm of   life is   past;
All   my trust on Thee is stayed, All   my help from Thee I   bring;
Thou of   life the fountain   art;   Free - ly   let   me take of   Thee:

Safe in - to   the ha - ven guide—O   re-ceive my soul at last!
Cov - er   my de - fence-less head With   the shad-ow of Thy win;.
Spring Thou up with-in   my   heart, Rise   to   all   e - ter - ni - ty.

No. 8.   Get You Ready.

P. B.   *P. Bilhorn.*

1. There's no hope be-yond the grave, my brother, Get you read-y for the
2. There's a life be-yond this life of sor-row, Get you read-y for the
3. Would you spend e-ter-ni-ty in heav-en, Get you read-y for the

coming of the Lord; In the blindness of thy sin-ning go no
coming of the Lord; He may sum-mon you to come to Him to-
coming of the Lord; To re-deem you Je-sus' pre-cious blood was

fur-ther, Get you read-y for the com-ing of the Lord.
mor-row, Get you read-y for the com-ing of the Lord.
giv-en, Get you read-y for the com-ing of the Lord.

CHORUS.

Get you read-y, get you read-y, Get you read-y for the coming of the Lord;

Rit.

Get you read-y, get you read-y, Get you ready for the coming of the Lord.

No. 9. No Night in Heaven.

Rev. 22: 5.

Alfred Beirly.

1. No night shall be in heav-en; no gath-'ring gloom Shall
2. No night shall be in heav-en; no dread-ful hour Of
3. No night shall be in heav-en, but end-less noon; No

o'er that glo-rious landscape ev-er come; No tears shall fall in
men-tal darkness of the tempter's power; A-cross those skies no
fast de-clin-ing sun, no wan-ing moon: But there the Lamb shall

sadness o'er those flow'rs That breathe their fragrance thro' celestial bow'rs.
en-vious clouds shall roll To dim the sun-light of the raptured soul.
ev-er shed His light, 'Mid pastures green and waters ev-er bright.

REFRAIN.

No night, no night shall be in heaven;
No night, no night

No night, no night shall be in heaven.
No night, no night

Thou art Drifting.

P. B.

P. Bilhorn,

1. Thou art drift-ing down life's riv - er, Drift - ing t'ward a sea,
2. At its mouth lie rocks tre-men - dous, Black - er than de-spair,
3. Hark! the wild white waves are foaming, Hun - gry, fierce and bold,
4. But be-yond these rag-ing bil - lows Lies a hap - py shore,
5. Oh! my friend, thy bark shall nev - er Reach that hap - py shore,
6. Call Him with en - treat - y ur - gent, Call Him near thy side,

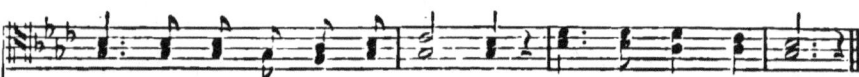

From whose shore no bark re - turn - eth, 'Tis E - ter - ni - ty.
Many a no - ble bark, my broth - er, Has been shipwrecked there.
O'er the shattered ves - sel dash - ing, Dread-ful, i - cy, cold.
Where the saints, redeem'd thro' Je - sus, Dwell for - ev - er - more.
Till the Lord becomes your Pi - lot; He will guide thee o'er.
Then o'er roughest, dark-est bil - lows, Safe - ly thou shalt glide.

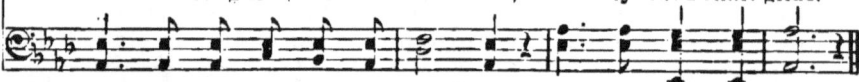

CHORUS. ff   f   m

Thou art drifting, thou art drifting, Drift-ing to E - 'ter - ni - ty;

ff   f   m

Thou art drifting, thou art drifting, Drift-ing to E - ter - ni - ty.

No. 11.

Go Forth! Go Forth!

L. E. Jones.   *P. Bilhorn.*

1. The field is great, the grain is white, The day is fad - ing in - to
2. Go forth and reap with will-ing hands, The gold-en grain a - wait-ing
3. Go forth! the la - bor - ers are few, There's much for willing hands to

night; Go forth! go forth, nor i - dle be, The Lord of
stands! Go forth, ye men, and gar - ner in The wand'ring
do:.... Go, men of faith, do not de - lay! The Mas - ter

Rit.   CHORUS.

har - vest need-eth thee. }
ones from paths of sin } Go forth! go forth and reap to-
bids you haste a - way. }

day, The field is read - y, haste a - way: Go forth, some

Rit.

pre - cious soul to win. Go bid them quick-ly en - ter in.

No. 12. Whiter than Snow.

James Nicholson.   Wm. G. Fischer.

1 Lord Je - sus, I long to be per-fect - ly whole; I want Thee for-
2. Lord Je - sus, look down from Thy throne in the skies, And help me to
3. Lord Je - sus, for this I most hum-bly en - treat; I wait, bless-ed
4. Lord Je - sus, Thou seest I pa-tient-ly wait; Come now, and with-

ev - er to live in my soul; Break down ev - 'ry i - dol, cast
make a com-plete sac - ri - fice; I give up my - self, and what-
Lord, at Thy cru - ci - fied feet, By faith for my clean-sing, I
in me a new heart cre - ate; To those who have sought Thee, Thou

out ev - 'ry foe; Now wash me, and I shall be whit - er than snow.
ev - er I know, Now wash me, and I shall be whit - er than snow.
see Thy blood flow-Now wash me, and I shall be whit - er than snow.
nev - er said'st No, Now wash me, and I shall be whit - er than snow.

CHORUS.

Whit - er than snow, yes, whit - er than snow; Now

wash me, and I shall be whit - er than snow.

No. 13.   Jesus is Coming Again.

Jessie E. Strout.   *P. Bilhorn.*

1. Lift up your voic-es, oh, loud let them ring, Je-sus is
2. Ech-o it, hill-top! pro-claim it, ye plain! Je-sus is
3. Sound it old o-cean, in might-i-est wave! Je-sus is
4. Soon we'll be wing-ing our flight thro' the air, Je-sus is

coming a-gain; Cheer up, ye pilgrims, be joy-ful and sing,
coming a-gain; Com-ing in glo-ry, the Lamb that was slain,
coming a-gain; Tell to the is-lands and shores that ye lave,
coming a-gain; Meet our Be-lov-ed, His glo-ry to share,

For Je-sus is com-ing a-gain.

Chorus.

Je-sus is com-ing, is com-ing a-gain, Je-sus is com-ing a-gain; Com-ing in glo-ry for-ev-er to reign, Je-sus is com-ing a-gain.

No. 14. Give Me the Wings of Faith.

Rev. I. Watts. 1700. Arr.

1. Give me the wings of faith to rise With-in the vail, and see
2. Once they were mourners here be-low, And pour'd out cries and tears:
3. I asked them whence their 'ict'ry came: They with u - nit - ed breath,

The saints a - bove, how great their joys, How bright their glories be.
They wrestled hard, as we do now, With sins, and doubts, and fears.
As-cribed their con-quest to the Lamb, Their tri-umph to His death.

Chorus.

Ma-ny are the friends who are waiting to-day, Happy on the golden strand,

Ma-ny are the voic-es calling us a-way, To join their glorious band.

Repeat pp.

Call-ing us a-way, Call-ing us a-way, Call-ing to the bet-ter land.

No. 15.   In Everything Give Thanks.

Julia H. Johnston.   P. Bilhorn.

1. Give thanks in the night of thy sor - row, Re-joice in thy
2. Re - joice in a fin - ished sal - va - tion, A cov - e - nant
3. In all the fair days of clear shin - ing Look up to the
4. No e - vil can ev - er be - tide us, If God be our

por - tion of pain, There dawneth a bright - er to-mor - row, Thy
or - dered and sure, Oh! dread not the hour of temp-ta - tion, For
source of thy light; When comforts and hopes are de-clin - ing, Re-
help and our shield, The love that re-deemed us will guide us, And

CHORUS

loss shall bring in - fi - nite gain. ⎞
"bless - ed are they that en - dure." ⎟ Give thanks un - to God and be
joice in the strength of His might. ⎟
mer - cy shall still be re - vealed. ⎠

joy - ful, What-ev - er may dai - ly be - fall, Re-joice in the Lord,

thy Re - deem - er, Who rul - eth su - preme o - ver all.

Henry F. Lyte.

Spanish. Arr. by E. M. H.

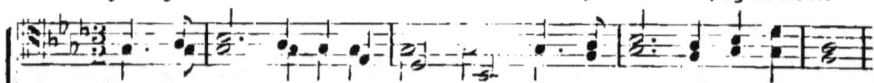

1. Je - sus, I my cross have ta - ken, All to leave and fol-low Thee,
2. Let the world despise and leave me, They have left my Sav-ior too;
3. Haste then on from grace to glo - ry, Arm'd by faith, and wing'd by pray'r!

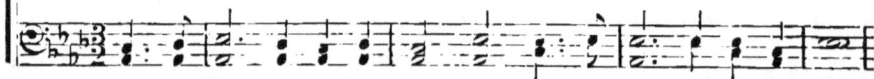

Na - ked, poor, despised, for-sa - ken, Thou from hence my all shalt be;
Human hearts and looks deceive me—Thou art not like them un-true;
Heav'n's e - ternal day's before thee, God's own hand shall guide thee there;

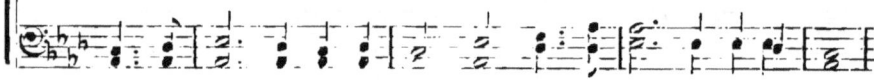

Per-ish ev - 'ry fond am - bi - tion, All I've sought, or hoped, or known,
Oh! while Thou dost smile upon me, God of wis-dom, love, and might,
Soon shall close thy earthly mis - sion, Soon shall pass thy earthly days,

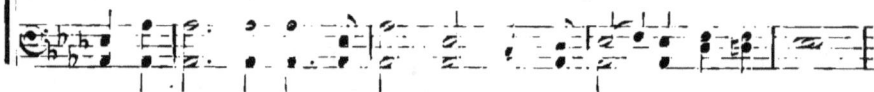

Yet how rich is my con - di - tion, God and heav'n are still my own.
Foes may hate, and friends disown me, Show Thy face, and all is bright.
Hope shall change to glad fru - i - tion, Faith to sight, and pray'r to praise.

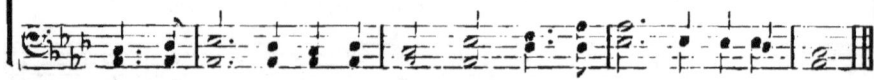

No. 17.   He Giveth Power to the Faint.

Julia H. Johnston.   P. Bilhorn.

1. Hast thou not known, hast thou not heard, That God, the Lord of all,
2. Lift up your eyes, be-hold on high, The ra-diant worlds a-far;
3. His word di-vine shall be thy guide, His love a sweet constraint;

Who fail-eth not nor wea-ry grows, Up-hold-eth all that fall?
His word is pledged that none shall fail, He nam-eth ev-'ry star.
O trust in Him who giv-eth grace And pow-er to the faint.

O sore-ly tried and trou-bled heart, To Him bring thy com-plaint;
O doubt-ing heart, in faith draw nigh, The children's por-tion claim;
Wait thou on God, the Source, a-lone, Whence all thy comfort springs;

To wea-ry ones He giv-eth strength, And pow'r un-to the faint.
He hath re-deemed from sin and death, He call-eth thee by name.
And thus thou shalt thy strength re-new, And mount on ea-gle's wings.

Blessed Jesus, Keep Me White.

P. B.

P. Bilhorn.

1. Bless-ed Je - sus, Thou art mine, All I have is whol-ly Thine;
2. I am safe with-in the fold, All my cares on Thee are roll'd;
3. Pre-cious Je - sus, day by day, Keep me in the ho-ly way;

Thou dost dwell with-in my heart, Make me clean in ev - 'ry part.
I en - joy the sweetest rest, For I'm lean-ing on Thy breast.
Keep my mind in per-fect peace, Ev-'ry day my faith in-crease.

Chorus.

white, ...

Bless-ed Je - - - sus, keep me white, keep me white, Keep me
Bless - ed Je - sus. keep me white,

walk - - - ing in the light......... All I have....... is
Keep me walking in the light, All I have

whol - ly Thine,........... Bless-ed Je - - - sus, Thou art mine.
is whol-ly Thine, Bless-ed Je - sus,

The Lily of the Valley.

English Melody.

1. I have found a friend in Je-sus, He's ev-'rything to me, He's the
2. He all my griefs has taken, and all my sorrows borne: In temp-
3. He will nev-er, nev-er leave me, nor yet for-sake me here, While I

fair-est of ten thousand to my soul: The Lil-y of the Val-ley, in
tation He's my strong and mighty tow'r: I have all for Him forsaken, and
live by faith and do His blesed will; A wall of fire a-bout me, I've

D. S. Lil-y of the Val-ley, the

FINE.

Him a - lone I see All I need to cleanse and make me fully whole.
all my i-dols torn From my heart, and now he keeps me by His pow'r.
noth-ing now to fear, With His manna He my hungry soul shall fill.

bright and Morning Star, He's the fair-est of ten thousand to my soul.

In sor-row He's my com-fort, in troub-le He's my stay,
Tho' all the world for-sake me, and Sa-tan tempts me sore,
Then sweeping up to glo-ry, to see His bless-ed face,

D. S.

He tells me ev-'ry care on Him to roll. He's the
Thro' Je-sus I shall safe-ly reach the goal. He's the
Where riv-ers of de-light shall ev-er roll. He's the

Hal-le-lu-jah!

No. 20. Waiting for the Savior.

Rev. G. W. Crofts. P. Bilhorn.

1. We are wait-ing for the Sav-ior, As the watch-er waits the light.
2. We are wait-ing for the Sav-ior, For our hearts are sick of sin.
3. We are wait-ing for the Sav-ior, In our sor-row and our grief.
4. We are wait-ing for the Sav-ior, For the night comes on a-pace;

When the sun in all his glo-ry Drives a - way the shades of night;
And there's no one here to heal us Of the pain we feel with-in;
Wait-ing for the great Con-sol - er, Who will bring a sweet re-lief;
Long-er grow the som-ber shad-ows 'Round our earthly dwell-ing-place.

We are wait-ing, on - ly wait-ing, For the Mas-ter to ap-pear.
There is no one but the Sav-ior, Who can cleanse the guilt-y soul.
Who will give for all our mourning, Oil of His a-bound-ing joy;
Soon we'll take the hap-py jour-ney, On the bright and shin-ing sea;

Waiting for the Savior.—Concluded.

CHORUS.

We are wait - - ing, We are watch - - ing,
We are wait-ing for our Sav - ior, We are watch-ing for our King,

We are read - y for the Mas - ter to ap - pear, (to ap-pear,)

We are wait - - - ing, We are watch - - - ing,
We are wait-ing for our Sav - ior, We are watch-ing for our King,

For the com - ing of our Lord is draw - ing near. (drawing near.)

No. 21. Soon will the Mist Roll Away.

Geo. Cooper.   H. M.

1. Yon-der's the land where the lov'd ones are, Soon will the mist roll a-
2. Dark looms the path, but the prom-ise heed, Soon will the mist roll a-
3. Bear thou the Cross till the Crown is won, Soon will the mist roll a-

way! Joy   soon   to   rest   in   that realm   a - far,
way! Je - sus a - lone can   re - lieve   thy   need,
way! Work till the   will   of   the   Lord   be   done,

Soon will the mist roll a - way! There in the lov-ing smile of
Soon will the mist roll a - way! Clear will the pur-pose of the
Soon will the mist roll a - way! All   will be rec - on - ciled to

Je - sus   to   bide, Vis-ions of glo-ry day by day!
Lord be   to thee, Hast-en the Mas-ter to o - bey;
thee   by and by, Faith guid-eth on   to per-fect day;

Soon will the Mist Roll Away.—Concluded.

Faith fond - ly whis - pers, while in shad - ows we hide,
Bliss - ful the vis - ion that be - yond we shall see,
Soon shall the glo - ry dawn up - on ev - 'ry eye,

Soon will the mist roll a - way!
Soon will the mist roll a - way!
Soon will the mist roll a - way!

REFRAIN.

Yon-der's the land where the lov'd ones are, Soon will the mist roll a - way! Joy soon to rest in that realm a - far, Soon will the mist roll a - way!

No. 22. By the Cross of Christ I Glory.

P. Bilhorn.   A. Beirly.

1. By the cross of Christ, our Sav-ior, We thro' faith are jus-ti-fied
2. By the cross we're lift-ed near-er To the heart of Him who died;
3. By the cross of Christ, our longings For a crown are sat-is-fied;
4. By the cross a fount of heal-ing Flowed from out His wounded side;

From all guilt and con-dem-na-tion, While we trust the Cru-ci-fied.
Dai-ly grows our vis-ion clear-er To be-hold the Cru-ci-fied.
Tho'ts of joy be-yond are thronging As we stand the cross be-side.
Sin-ners, there in mer-cy kneeling, Seek ye now the Cru-ci-fied.

God for-bid............ that we should glo-ry Save in

CHORUS.

God for-bid that we should glo-ry

Je - - sus' cross a-lone:........ For His blood...... still tells the

Save in Je-sus' cross a-lone; For His blood still

sto-ry, How for sin........... He did a-tone.

tells the sto-ry, How for sin He did a-tone. (a-tone.)

When My Savior I Shall See.

Arr. P. B.
P. Bilhorn.

1. When my Sav - ier I shall see, In His glo-rious like-ness be,
2. When I'm whol-ly freed from sin, Spotless, clean and pure within,
3. When my feet shall press the shore, Trod by an-gel's feet be-fore,
4. Oh, till then be this my care, More His im-age blest to bear;

Clad in robes by love sup-plied, Then shall I be sat-is-fied.
Meet to stand by Je-sus' side, Then shall I be sat-is-fied.
Near to liv-ing streams that glide, Then shall I be sat-is-fied.
More to con-quer self and pride, So shall I be sat-is-fied.

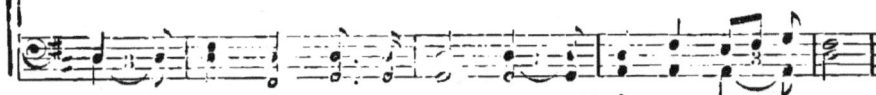

CHORUS.

Sat-is-fi-ed with love di-vine, Sat-is-fied, since Christ is mine,

Ev-'ry need in Him supplied, Then shall I be sat-is-fied.

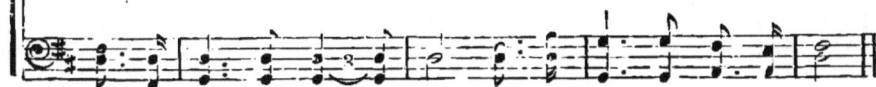

No. 24. A Story Sweet and True.

E. W. Oakes.   P. Bilhorn.

1. We'll sing the won-drous sto - ry, 'Tis ev - er sweet and true;
2. The cru - el world, they took Him, With thorns they crowned His head;
3. His friends whom He loved dear - ly, And whom He died to save,
4. My Lord now reigns in glo - ry, He's com - ing soon for me;

Of Je - sus' love so pre - cious, Now free - ly of - fered you;
And then to Cal-vary's mountain The pre - cious Lamb was led;
They begged His pre - cious bod - y, And laid it in the grave;
And then with all the ran - somed, His glo - rious face I'll see;

He left the joys of heav - en, His Fa - ther's home on high,
The nails of shame were driv - en, The blood flowed from His side;
But God, His Fa - ther, raised Him Tri-umph - ant from the dead;
And shout, be-hold the Bride-groom, Put on your gar - ments fair,

For lost and ru - in'd sin - ners, To suf - fer and to die.
He cried, "O God, for - give them," And bowed His head and died.
Oh! glo - ry hal - le - lu - jah! Now death is cap - tive led.
And go ye out to meet Him, With rap - ture in the air.

The Lord's Our Rock!

V. J. C.   *P. Bilhorn.*

1. The Lord's our Rock, in Him we hide; A shel-ter in the time of storm!
2. A shade by day, de-fence by night, A shel-ter in the time of storm!
3. The rag-ing storm may round us beat, A shel-ter in the time of storm!
4. O Rock di-vine, O Ref-uge dear, A shel-ter in the time of storm!

Se-cure what-ev-er ill be-tide, A shel-ter in the time of storm!
No fears a-larm, no foes af-fright, A shel-ter in the time of storm!
We'll nev-er leave our safe re-treat, A shel-ter in the time of storm!
Be Thou our Help-er, ev-er near, A shel-ter in the time of storm!

CHORUS.

Oh, Je-sus is the Rock in a wea-ry land, A

wea-ry land, a wea-ry land, Oh, Je-sus is the

Rock in a wea-ry land, A shel-ter in the time of storm.

No. 26. Onward, Christian Soldiers.

S. Baring-Gould.   *Sullivan. Arr. by E. M. H.*

1. On - ward, Chris-tian sol - diers, March - ing as to war,
2. Like a might - y ar - my, Moves the Church of God:
3. Crowns and thrones may per - ish, King - doms rise and wane,
4. On - ward, then, ye faith - ful, Join our hap - py throng,

With the cross of Je - sus Go - ing on be - fore:
Broth - ers, we are tread - ing Where the saints have trod:
But the Church of Je - sus Con - stant will re - main;
Blend with ours your voic - es, In the tri - umph song:

Christ, the roy - al Mas - ter, Leads a - gainst the foe;
We are not di - vid - ed, All one bod - y we,
Gates of hell can nev - er 'Gainst that Church pre - vail;
Glo - ry, laud, and hon - or, Un - to Christ the King:

For - ward in - to bat - tle, See, His ban - ners go.
One in hope and doc - trine, One in char - i - ty.
We have Christ's own prom - ise, And that can - not fail.
This, thro' count - less a - ges, Men and an - gels sing.

Chorus.

On - ward, Chris-tian sol - diers, March - ing as to war,

Onward, Christian Soldiers.—Concluded.

With the cross of Je - sus Go - ing on be - fore.

No. 27. **Go in Peace.**

Julia H. Johnston. *P. Bilhorn.*

1. Oh, who is this for - giv - eth sin, And prom - is - es re -
2. "Thy faith hath saved thee," gra - cious word! Let fear and doubt-ing
3. Ac - cord - ing to Thy faith in Him, Thy com - fort shall in -
4. A - long the com - mon ways of life Till ev'n - ing brings re -
5. For - giv - en much, oh, love Him much, Thou sin - ner saved by

lease? The voice of Je - sus speaks with - in, And
cease; O - be - dient to thy might - y Lord, Look
crease, Let not thy hope and trust grow dim, Be -
lease, A - mid the dai - ly toil and strife, He
grace, If thou hast felt His heal - ing touch, Thou

whis - pers, "Go in peace," And whis - pers, "Go in peace."
up and go in peace, Look up and go in peace.
lieve and go in peace, Be - lieve and go in peace.
bids thee go in peace, He bids thee go in peace.
shalt be - hold His face, Thou shalt be - hold His face.

No. 28. I Could Not Do Without Thee.

Thalberg. Arr.

1. I could not do with-out Thee, O Sav-ior of the ' st.
2. I could not do with-out Thee, I can-not stand a lone.
3. I could not do with-out Thee, For years are fleet-ing

Whose pre-cious blood re-deemed me At such tre-men-dous cost;
I have no strength or good-ness, No wis-dom of my own;
And soon in sol-emn si-lence The riv-er must be passed;

Thy right-eous-ness, Thy par-don, Thy pre-cious blood must be
But Thou, be-lov-ed Sav-ior, Art all in all to me,
But Thou wilt nev-er leave me, And tho' the waves roll high,

My on-ly hope and com-fort, My glo-ry and my plea.
And weak-ness will be pow-er, If lean-ing hard on Thee.
I know Thou wilt be near me, And whis-per, "It is I."

No. 29. Cast All Your Care Upon Him.

The "Lanan."
Slowly.

P. Bilhorn.

1. Oh, why do you car-ry your bur-den a-lone, That bur-den of sor-row and care? Since Je-sus is say-ing in ten-der-est tone, "Your-self and your bur-den I'll bear."

2. Then go tell Him your troub-le, He'll give you re-lief, If on Him you'll on-ly de-pend; To cries of His chil-dren He'll nev-er be deaf, If on-ly in faith they as-cend.

3. If sick-ness dis-tress you, or pain, He will heal, Or else give you strength to en-dure; To Je-sus who suf-fered, then fer-vent-ly kneel, And trust ing-ly ask Him to cure.

4. Then go to Him al-ways, what-ev-er be-fall, Of sick-ness or sor-row or sin; Tell Je-sus your troub-le, and tell to Him all, And then let your prais-es be-gin.

CHORUS. m

Come cast all thy care on Je-sus, Oh, wea-ry and troubled soul, Come cast all thy bur-den up-on Him; He wants not a part but the whole.

No. 30.　　　A Happy Band Are We.

P. B.

P Bilhorn.

1. We're a hap-py Christian band, March-ing to the heav'nly land!
2. 'Tis a bright and cheerful way, When the Sav-ior we o-bey!
3. What a glo-rious morn 'twill be When our loved ones we shall see!
4. Come, and join us, one and all, Heed the Sav-ior's lov-ing call;

'Tis the Sav-ior leads us there To the Fa-ther's home so fair!
By His lov-ing hand we're led, By His pre-cious man-na fed!
When with Je-sus we shall reign, Nev-er-more to part a-gain!
Turn from sin and seek the Lord, He will save you! Trust His word.

CHORUS.

Come, and join.......... our Chris-tian band,

Come, and join our Chris-tian band, Christian band,

On re-demp - - - tion's ground we stand!

On re-demp-tion's ground we stand, we stand!

We are ran - - - somed, we are free,

We are ransomed, we are free, we are free,

A Happy Band Are We.—Concluded.

Rit.

Sing His praise.......... e - ter - nal - ly.

Sing His praise e - ter - nal - ly, e - ter - nal - ly.

No. 31.   **Sun of My Soul.**

John Keble, 1827.   P. Bilhorn.

1. Sun of my soul, Thou Sav - ior dear, It is not
2. When the soft dews of kind - ly sleep, My wea - ried
3. A - bide with me from morn till eve, For with - out
4. Watch by the sick; en - rich the poor With bless - ings
5. Come near and bless us when we wake, Ere thro' the

night if Thou be near; Oh, may no earth - born
eye - lids gen - tly steep, Be my last tho't, how
Thee I can - not live; A - bide with me when
from Thy bound - less store; Be ev - 'ry mourn - er's
world our way we take; Till in the o - cean

Rit.

cloud a - rise, To hide Thee from Thy ser - vant's eyes.
sweet to rest For - ev - er on my Sav - ior's breast.
night is nigh, For with - out Thee I dare not die.
sleep to - night, Like in - fant's slum - bers, pure and light.
of Thy love We lose our - selves in heav'n a - bove.

No. 32. Rally Round the Cross.

E. F. M. E. F. Miller.

1. Again we have come in Jehovah's name, The bat-tle to fight and the
2. When Israel of old march'd around the wall, They blew with their trumpets and
3. Our Fa-thers, we know, to the Lord were true, They took up the sword and they
4. We all must engage if a crown we'd wear, And yonder with Je-sus the
5. The conflict will soon be for-ev-er o'er, The sum-mons will come from the

vic-t'ry gain, We'll gird on the ar-mor and to the con-flict go,
shout-ed all; Then down came the walls, and they took the mighty k'ng;
bat-tled thro'; They're safe now in glo-ry and look-ing down to-night,
glo-ry share; Then let all be true as we in-to bat-tle go,
oth-er shore; And then home to glo-ry re-joic-ing we will go,

And in the name of Je-sus we'll con-quer ev-'ry foe.
To God they gave the glo-ry, who did sal-va-tion bring.
They call to you and me to be faith-ful in the fight.
And res-cue ev-'ry sin-ner from death and all its woe.
To praise Him for the vic-'try He gave us here be-low.

CHORUS.

Then ral-ly! ral-ly! ral-ly round the cross! No one ev-er

Rally Round the Cross.—Concluded.

there will suffer loss; And in the name of Je-sus we'll face the deadly foe,

And vic - to - ry will perch up - on our ban - ner as we go.

No. 33. **Holy Spirit, Faithful Guide.**

M. M. W.

M. M. Wells.

FINE.

1. { Ho - ly Spir - it, faith - ful Guide, Ev - er near the Christian's side.
   { Gen - tly lead us by the hand, Pil-grims in a des - ert land;

2. { Ev - er pres - ent, tru - est Friend, Ev - er near, Thine aid to lend.
   { Leave us not to doubt and fear, Grop-ing on in darkness drear.

3. { When our days of toil shall cease, Wait-ing still for sweet re-lease.
   { Noth-ing left but heav'n and pray'r, Wond'ring if our names are there;

D.C. Whisp'ring soft-ly, wand'rer, come! Fol - low me, I'll guide thee home.
D.C. Whis-per soft - ly, wand'rer, come! Fol - low me, I'll guide thee home.
D.C. Whis-per soft - ly, wand'rer, come! Fol - low me, I'll guide thee home.

D. C.

Wea - ry souls for - e'er re - joice, While they hear that sweetest voice,
When the storms are rag - ing sore, Hearts grow faint, and hopes give o'er;
Wad - ing deep the dis - mal flood, Plead-ing naught but Je - sus' blood;

No. 34.   **Love, Rest, Peace and Joy.**

P. B.

P. Bilhorn.

1. There is love, true love, in the heav'n-ly home, Ma-ny
2. There is rest, sweet rest, in the home of God; 'Tis the
3. There is peace, sweet peace, in the home a - bove; For we'll
4. There is joy, glad joy, in the land of song, For in

dear ones there have gone, To be free from care, here no more to roam.
rest that Christ doth give, To the souls who trust in His precious blood.
know no heart-breaks there; Sorrow ne'er shall come, 'tis a home of love.
heav'n we all shall sing: We are near-ing home soon to join the throng.

CHORUS.

There is love,   there is

They have joined that hap - py throng.)
They for - ev - er - more shall live.)
Of that peace we all may share. }   There is love,
In the pres - ence of our King.)

rest.   there is peace.   there is joy.

there is rest.   there is peace.   there is joy, In that

land of song, where the loved have gone. There is love, rest, peace and joy.

Glad Tidings of Joy.

W. A. O.

W. A. Ogden.

1. O Zi - on that bring - est good ti - dings, Lift up your glad
2. O Zi - on that bring - est good ti - dings, The Bridegroom is
3. O Zi - on that bring - est good ti - dings, The hope of the

voice to the skies, Go pub-lish sal - va - tion thro' Je - sus, Bid
com - ing this way, Go forth in thy splendor to meet Him, A-
world is in thee, Pro-claim to the sin - ner sal - va - tion, And

CHORUS.

na - tions from darkness a - rise. Go tell............ the glad
rise in thy beau - ty to - day. Go tell the glad ti-dings, glad
bid him from bondage go free.

ti - dings, The won - - - - der - ful ti - dings, Glad
ti - dings, The won - der - ful, won - der - ful ti - dings,

tidings of joy, Glad ti-dings of joy, Go tell the glad tidings of joy.

No. 36. To Save a Poor Sinner Like Me.

Rev. John O. Foster, A. M.　　　　　　　　　　　　　Grace I. Foster.

1. I'll sing of the sto-ry, how Je-sus from glo-ry Has
2. His glo-ry im-mor-tal bright o-ver the por-tal, Has
3. Tho' sea-sons of er-ror and mo-ments of ter-ror, Like
4. My peace like a riv-er flows on-ward for-ev-er, A

saved a poor sin-ner like me: That all who be-lieve Him and
ban-ished the gloom from the grave; The Lord has as-cend-ed, the
bil-lows of sor-row may roll; In Christ I'm con-fid-ing, in
tide to e-ter-ni-ty's sea, To swell the old sto-ry with

all who re-ceive Him, His bless-ed sal-va-tion may see.
dark-ness is end-ed And now He is might-y to save.
Him I am hid-ing, With safe-ty and rest to my soul.
voic-es in glo-ry, He saved a poor sin-ner like me.

CHORUS.

Then sing the glad cho-rus, His ban-ner is o'er us, His

mer-cy is boundless and free, From heav-en de-scend-ed, His

To Save a Poor Sinner Like Me.—Concluded.

love is ex-tend-ed. To save a poor sin-ner like me.

No. 37. 'Twas Jesus My Savior.

P. Bilhorn.

1. 'Twas Je-sus My Sav-ior, who died on the tree, To o-pen a
2. And when I was will-ing with all things to part, He gave me my
3. And with all the ransom'd by Je-sus, my Head, From glo-ry to
4. Come, sin-ner, to Je-sus, no long-er de-lay, A full, free sal-

fount-ain for sin-ners like me; The blood of that fount-ain wher-
boun-ty, His love in my heart; So now I am joined to the
glo-ry I then shall be led; I'll fall at His feet, and His
va-tion He of-fers to-day; Ac-cept it just now, and in

ev-er it flows, It cleans-es the vil-est, and par-don be-stows.
son-quer-ing band, And marching to glo-ry at Je-sus' command.
mer-cy a-dore, And sing of the blood of the cross ev-er-more.
Je-sus be-lieve, The life ev-er-last-ing you then shall re-ceive.

No. 38.   **Junior Endeavor Hymn.**

Rev. S. S. Cryor.   *P. Bilhorn.*

Melody in 2d Tenor.

1. We are com-ing, lov-ing Sav-ior, At Thy blest com-mand;
2. We are on-ly vol-un-teers, Read-y to o-bey;
3. Help us in our hearts to con-quer All our foes, and be
4. May the church—Thy glo-rious ar-my—Find our shep-herd sling

We would join Thy might-y ar-my, With our jun-ior band.
Bless-ed Sav-ior, be our Lead-er, Guide us day by day.
In the world's great field of bat-tle, Sol-diers true to Thee.
Might-y to de-stroy all gi-ants Who de-fy her King.

CHORUS.

On-ward then, we'll march to vic-t'ry, Joy-ful-ly we'll sing;

We will nev-er be dis-cour-aged: Je-sus is our King.

No. 39. Thy Love to Me.

Mrs. M. E. Gates.   *E. C. Avis.*

With expression.

1. Thy love to me, O Christ, Thy love to me,
2. Thy rec - ord I be - lieve, Thy word to me,
3. Im - mor - tal love of Thine, Thy sac - ri - fice,
4. Let me more clear - ly trace Thy love to me,

Not mine to Thee, I plead, Not mine to Thee!
Thy love I now re - ceive, Full, changeless, free:
In - fi - nite need of mine, On - ly sup - plies,
See in the Fa - ther's face His love for thee;

This is my com - fort strong, This is my on - ly song,
Love from the sin - less Son, Love to the sin - ful one,
Streams of di - vin - est pow'r Flow to me ev - 'ry hour,
Know as He loves the Son, So dost thou love thine own:

Thy love, O Christ, to me, Thy love to me.

No. 40. Singing as We Journey to Zion.

Ada Blenkhorn.

P. Bilhorn.

1. We'll watch and pray and la-bor ev-'ry day, Singing as we jour-ney to
2. With Christ as guide no e-vil can be-tide, Singing as we jour-ney to
3. With shield and sword we'll battle for the Lord, Singing as we jour-ney to
4. The vic-t'ry won, we'll glo-ri-fy the Son, Singing as we jour-ney to

Zi-on, Till He shall come to call His children home, Singing as we
Zi-on, We'll trust His grace till we behold His face, Singing as we
Zi-on, We'll trust our King, us vic-to-ry to bring, Singing as we
Zi-on, The "blood-wash'd throng" will welcome us ere long, Singing as we

journey to Zi-on. Look-ing to our Lord, trust-ing in His word,
journey to Zi-on. Love with-in our heart bids all fear de-part,
journey to Zi-on. Striv-ing for the right, put-ting foes to flight,
journey to Zi-on. Read-y! be our cry, when the Lord is nigh,

Marching when He bids us go for-ward; By His strong hand we'll
Win-ning oth-er souls for the Mas-ter; He's al-ways near our
Fol-low-ing our Guide where He leads us; By His great might we'll
Call-ing us to lay down our ar-mor, Our war-fare past, we'll

pass the Ca-naan land, Sing-ing as we jour-ney to Zi - on.
pil - grim way to cheer. Sing-ing as we jour-ney to Zi - on.
con - quer in the fight, Sing-ing as we jour-ney to Zi - on.
gath - er home at last, Sing-ing as we jour-ney to Zi - on.

No. 41.   Take My Life and Let it Be.

Frances R. Havergal.   Malan.

1. Take my life and let it be Con - se - cra - ted, Lord, to
2. Take my feet and let them be Swift and beau - ti - ful for
3. Take my lips and let them be Fill'd with mes - sa - ges for
4. Take my mo - ments and my days, Let them flow in end - less

Thee: Take my hands and let them move At the im-pulse
Thee; Take my voice and let me sing Al - ways, on - ly,
Thee; Take my sil - ver and my gold, Not a mite would
praise; Take my in - tel - lect and use Ev - 'ry pow'r as

of Thy love, At the im - pulse of Thy love.
for my King, Al - ways, on - ly, for my King.
I with - hold, Not a mite would I with - hold.
Thou shalt choose, Ev - 'ry pow'r as Thou shalt choose.

No. 42.

Who Will Go?

Rev. D. March.   *P. Bilhorn.*

1. Hark! the voice of Je - sus cry-ing, "Who will go and work to - day?
2. If you can - not cross the o - cean, And the hea-then lands ex-plore,
3. If you can - not speak like an - gels, If you can-not preach like Paul,
4. If a-mong the old - er peo - ple, You may not be apt to teach;
5. Let none hear you i - dly say-ing, "There is noth-ing I can do,"

Fields are white and har-vest wait-ing, Who will bear the sheaves a-way?"
You can find the hea-then near - er, You can find them at your door.
You can tell the love of Je - sus, You can say He died for all.
"Feed my lambs," said Christ, our Shepherd, "Place the food within our reach."
While the souls of men are dy - ing, And the Mas - ter calls for you.

Loud and strong the Mas-ter call - eth, Rich re - ward He of - fers thee;
If you can - not give your thousands, You can give the wid-ow's mite,
If you can - not rouse the wick - ed With the judgment's dread a-larms,
And it may be that the chil-dren You have led with trembling hand,
Take the task He gives you glad - ly, Let His work your pleas-ure be;

Who will an-swer, glad - ly say - ing, "Here am I;" send me, send me."
And the least you do for Je - sus, Will be pre-cious in His sight.
You can lead the lit - tle chil-dren To the Sav - ior's wait-ing arms.
Will be found a-mong your jew - els, When you reach the bet - ter land
An - swer quickly when He call-eth, "Here am I; send me, send me!"

No. 43.   Drinking at the Living Fountain.

P. H. Roblin.   *P. Bilhorn.*

1. I have found a balm for all my woe,   Je-sus is the liv-ing fountain;
2. When I came to Je - sus in my sin, Bending at the liv-ing fountain;
3. As I heard His voice so kind and sweet, Sounding at the liv-ing fountain.
4. To the fount-ain come, O come to - day, Flowing is the liv-ing fountain;

  I am full of joy, as Christ I know, Drinking at the fount of life.
Then He heard my pray'r and made me clean, Cleans'd me at the fount of life.
Then I wept and sang low at His feet, Drinking at the fount of life.
  If you come He'll wash your sins a - way,   Je-sus is the fount of life.

Chorus.

O the fount is Christ, in Him be - lieve, Drinking at the liv-ing fountain;

All who come to Him the life re - ceive, Je-sus is the fount of life.

No. 44. I'm Bound to Enter Heaven.

Miss A. Blenkhorn.　　　　　　　　　　*Miss A. Blenkhorn. Arr. by P. P.*

1. The Sav-ior gave His life for me, I'm bound to en-ter heav-en:
2. O, brother, won't you come with me? I'm bound to en-ter heav-en:
3. He walks each rug-ged path with me, I'm bound to en-ter heav-en:
4. There waits for me a roy-al crown, I'm bound to en-ter heav-en;
5. To His own word He will be true, I'm bound to en-ter heav-en:

From Sa-tan's yoke He sets me free, I'm bound to en-ter heav-en.
To - day the Sav-ior call-eth thee, I'm bound to en-ter heav-en.
Each thorn-y path He'll walk with thee, I'm bound to en-ter heav-en.
When life's last bur-den I lay down, I'm bound to en-ter heav-en.
He'll keep a star-ry crown for you, O come and en-ter heav-en.

CHORUS.

Bound for the Ca-naan land, Bound for the Ca-naan land,

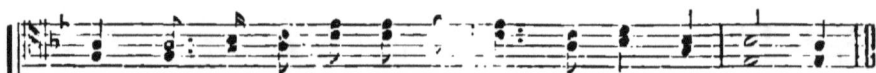

Bound for the Ca-naan land, I'm bound to en-ter heav-en.

No. 45.　　　How Firm a Foundation.

Geo. Keith.　　　(PORTUGUESE HYMN.)

1. How firm a foun - da - tion, ye saints of the Lord, Is laid for your
2. "Fear not, I am with thee, O be not dismayed, For I am thy
3. "When thro' the deep wa - ters I call thee to go, The riv - ers of
4. "The soul that on Je - sus hath lean'd for re - pose, I will not, I

faith in His ex - cel - lent word, What more can He say, than to
God, I will still give thee aid; I'll strengthen thee, help thee, and
sor - row shall not o - ver - flow; For I will be with thee the
will not de - sert to his foes; That soul, tho' all hell should en -

you He hath said, To you, who for ref - uge to Je - sus have
cause thee to stand, Up - held by my gra - cious, om - nip - o - tent
tri - als to bless, And sanc - ti - fy to thee thy deep - est dis -
deav - or to shake, I'll nev - er, no nev - er, no nev - er for -

fled? To you, who for ref - uge to Je - sus have fled?
hand, Up - held by my gra - cious, om - nip - o - tent hand."
tress, And sanc - ti - fy to thee thy deep - est dis - tress."
sake, I'll nev - er, no nev - er, no nev - er for - sake!"

No. 46.
Sweet Peace.

P. B.

P. Bilhorn.

1. There comes to my heart one sweet strain, (sweet strain,) A
2. By Christ on the cross peace was made, (was made,) My
3. When Je - sus as Lord I had crowned, (had crowned.) My
4. In Je - sus for peace I a - bide, (a - bide,) And

glad and a joy - ous re - frain, (re - frain,) I
debt by His death was all paid, (all paid.) No
heart with His peace did a - bound, (a - bound.) In
as I keep close to His side, (His side,) There's

sing it a - gain and a - gain, Sweet peace, the gift of God's love.
oth - er foun - da - tion is laid For peace, the gift of God's love.
Him the rich blessing I found, Sweet peace, the gift of God's love.
noth-ing but peace doth be - tide, Sweet peace, the gift of God's love.

CHORUS.

Peace, peace, sweet peace, Won-der-ful gift from a - bove, (a-bove,) Oh,

ff   *p*   *Rit.*

won-der-ful, won-der-ful peace, Sweet peace, the gift of God's love.

The Old Oaken Bucket.

Samuel Woodworth.

E. Kiallmark.
Arr. by. E. M. H.

Melody in 2d Tenor.

1. {
How dear to my heart are the scenes of my child-hood, When
The or-chard, the mead-ow, the deep-tan-gled wild-wood, And
}
D.C. The cot of my fa-ther, the dai-ry-house nigh it, And

2. {
That moss-cov-ered buck-et I hailed as a treas-ure, For
I found it the source of an ex-qui-site pleas-ure, The
}
D.C. Then soon with the em-blem of truth o-ver-flow-ing, And

CHO.—*The old oak-en buck-et, the i-ron-bound buck-et, The*

FINE.

fond rec-ol-lec-tion pre-sents them to view! }
ev-'ry loved spot which my in-fan-cy knew, }
e'en the rude buck-et that hung in the well.

oft-en at noon, when re-turned from the field, }
pur-est and sweet-est that na-ture can yield. }
drip-ping with cool-ness, it rose from the well.

moss-cov-er'd buck-et that hung in the well.

The wide, spreading pond, and the mill that stood by it, The
How ar-dent I seized it, with hands that were glow-ing, And

D. C.

bridge and the rock where the cat-a-ract fell;
quick to the white-peb-bled bot-tom it fell;

No. 48. The Savior is My All in All.

P. B.

Melody in 2d Tenor.

P. Bilhorn.

1. The Sav-ior is my all in all, He is my con-stant theme!
2. His Spir-it gives sweet peace with-in, And bids all care de - part;
3. And what-so-ev - er I may ask, To glo - ri - fy His Name,
4. Oh, praise the Lord, my soul, re-joice, Give thanks un-to thy God,

By sim-ply trust-ing in His word, He keeps me pure and clean.
He fills my soul with righteousness, And pu - ri - fies the heart.
The Fa-ther free-ly gives to me, Since Christ the Sav-ior came.
Who took thee in thy sin - ful - ness, And cleans'd thee by His blood!

CHORUS.

Glo - ry! oh, glo - ry! Je - sus hath re - deemed me;

Rit.

Glo - ry! oh, glo - ry! He washed my sins a - way! (a - way!)

No. 49.   Able to Save and Keep.

C. E. G.   P. Bilhorn.

1. He's a - ble to keep you from fall - ing, He's a - ble all
2. He's a - ble to heal our dis - eas - es, Our bod - ies, if
3. He's a - ble to car - ry our bur - dens, To rid us of
4. God's tho'ts to His chil - dren are pre - cious, All this and much

things to sub - due, To bind up the bro - ken in
maimed, He'll make whole; He's a - ble to keep us from
all anx - ious care; He's a - ble to rest us when
more will He give; Thro' faith in the dear name of

spir - it, And save to the ut - ter - most too.
sin - ning, And per - fect His life in the soul.
wea - ry, He's will - ing our cross - es to share.
Je - sus, We ask and thro' Him we re - ceive.

CHORUS.

A - - ble, will - - ing, a - ble and willing to save,

A-ble to save,   a - ble to keep,

A - - ble, will - - ing, Je - sus is a - ble to save.

A - ble to save,   a - ble to keep,

No. 50.   Conquer Through His Word.

Miss J. H. Johnston.   P. Bilhorn.

1. I've en - list - ed in the ar - my of the Lord, He has
2. 'Tis an ar - my that is ev - er sure to win; 'Tis the
3. There are foes on ev - 'ry hand who seek to harm, But with
4. Come and join this conqu'ring ar - my of the Lord; Let Him

arm'd me with a hel-met, shield and sword, Now to bat-tle for the right,
Lord who leads a-gainst the hosts of sin; Thro' the word that giveth light,
us there is an ev - er - last - ing arm; With our Captain in command,
give to you a hel-met, shield and sword; By the pow'r of Jesus' might,

by the pow'r of Jesus might, By His grace I'll con-quer thro' His word.
we shall conquer in the fight, Tho' the en - e - my be strong with-in,
we are strong in heart and hand, And secure a-gainst all false a - larm.
you may battle for the right, You may triumph thro' His roy - al word.

CHORUS.

Hal - le - lu - jah! Hal - le - lu - jah! Prais-es
Hal - le - lu - jah!   Hal - le - lu - jah!

Conquer Through His Word.—Concluded.

to His ev - erlasting name we'll sing, Hal-le - lu - - jah! Hal-le-
Hal - le - lu-jah!

lu - - jah!   We shall conquer thro' our Lord and King.
Hal - le - lu - jah!

No. 51.   Cheer Thee.
                                                        Arr.

1. God   is   near thee, Therefore cheer thee, Sad   soul,   sad   soul;
2. Calm thy sad - ness, Look in glad - ness, On   high,   on   high;
3. Mark the   sea - bird Wild-ly wheel-ing, Thro' skies, thro skies;
4. There-fore cheer thee, God is   near thee, Sad   soul,   sad soul;

He'll de-fend thee, When a-round thee Bil - lows roll. bil-lows roll.
Faint and wea - ry Pil-grim, cheer thee. Help is nigh, help is nigh.
God   defends him, God at - tends him When he cries, when he cries.
In   thy blindness, Trust His kindness, When storms roll o'er thy soul.

No. 52.   Ye Must be Born Again.

Rev. W. T. Sleeper.   *Geo. C. Stebbins. Arr.*

1. A rul - er once came un - to Je - sus by night, To
2. Ye chil - dren of men now at - tend to the word So
3. Oh, ye that would en - ter that glo - ri - ous rest, And
4. A dear one in heav - en thy heart yearns to see, And

ask Him the way to sal - va - tion and light, The Mas - ter made
sol - emn - ly ut - tered by Je - sus, the Lord, And let not the
sing with the ransom'd, the song of the blest, The life ev - er -
now at the gate may be wait - ing for thee, Then list to the

a - gain......

an - swer. in words true and plain, "Ye must be born, be born a-gain."
mes-sage to you be in vain, "Ye must be born, be born a-gain."
last - ing if ye would ob - tain, "Ye must be born, be born a-gain."
note of this sol - emn re - frain, "Ye must be born, be born a-gain."

a - gain......

CHORUS.   a - gain,.....

"Ye must be born a - gain,...... Ye must be born, be born a-gain, I
be born a-gain,

Ye Must be Born Again.—Concluded.

a - gain......

ver - i - ly, ver - i - ly, say un - to thee, Ye must be born, be born a-gain."

a - gain......

No. 53. ## Rock of Ages.

A. M. Toplady.   *Thos. Hastings.*

1. Rock of A - ges, cleft for me, Let me hide my - self in Thee;
2. Could my tears for - ev - er flow, Could my zeal no lan-guor know,
3. While I draw this fleet-ing breath, When my eyes shall close in death,

Let the wa - ter and the blood, From Thy wounded side which flowed,
These for sin could not a - tone; Thou must save, and Thou a - lone;
When I rise to worlds un-known, And be - hold Thee on Thy throne,

Be of sin the dou - ble cure, Save from wrath and make me pure.
In my hand no price I bring, Sim - ply to Thy cross I cling.
Rock of A - ges, cleft for me, Let me hide my - self in Thee.

God Will Help You Stand.

L. W. Lyon.   P. Bilhorn.

1. Tho' the way seems dark be - fore you, Broth - er, don't de - spair;
2. Is your heart depressed, my broth-er? Je - sus is your friend;
3. At your hearth-stone lov'd ones praying, Plead - ing for their son,
4. Ma - ny pray'rs for you are ris - ing To the throne of grace,

Bright - er light shall yet shine o'er you, In this world of care.
He will save you, He will lead you To your journey's end.
With a par - ent's sup - pli - ca - tion, For the way-ward one.
Can you still His love de - spis - ing, Turn from Him your face?

He who by His might-y pow - er, Holds the sea and land,
Do not fear to trust Him, broth-er, See His wound-ed hand;
Lov'd one, cast you sins be - hind you, Join the ran-somed band;
Broth - er, rise from sin and sor - row, Take thy Fa - ther's hand;

Still is near, tho' dark the hour, He will help you stand;
He has died for your re-demp-tion, He will help you stand;
Grace suf - fi - cient He will give you, He will help you stand;
Fear no doubt of sin to - mor-row, He will help you stand;

God Will Help You Stand.—Concluded.

Still is near, tho' dark the hour, He will help you stand.
He has died for your re-demp-tion, He will help you stand.
Grace suf-fi-cient He will give you, He will help you stand.
Fear no doubt of sin to-mor-row, He will help you stand.

CHORUS.

He will help you stand, He will help you stand.

Al-ways near, He'll not for-sake you, God will help you stand.

No. 55. He Knows.

P. Bilhorn.

Lento.

1. He knows the bit-ter, wea-ry, way, The end-less striv-ing day by day.
2. He knows when faint and worn we sink, How deep the pain, how near the brink
3. He knows! oh, tho't so full of bliss! For tho' on earth our joy we miss,
4. He knows! oh, heart, take up thy cross, And know earth's treasures are but dross,

Animated.

The souls that weep, the souls that pray, He knows! He knows! He knows!
Of dark de-spair, we pause and shrink, He knows! He knows! He knows!
We still can bear it, feel-ing this, He knows! He knows! He knows!
And all will prove as gain or loss! He knows! He knows! He knows!

No. 56. The Wayside Cross.

C. L. St. John.

Dr. H. R. Palmer.

Ad lib.

1. "Which way shall I take?" shouts a voice on the night, I'm a pil-grim a-
2. "Which way shall I take for the bright golden span That bridg-es the
3. "See the light from the palace in sil - ver - y lines, How they pencil the

ORGAN.

wea - ried and spent is my light; And I seek for the palace that
wa - ters so safe-ly for man? To the right? to the left? ah!
hedg - es and fruit-la - den vines— My fortune! my all! for

Slower and sustained. *Rit.*

rests on the hill, But be-tween us a stream li - eth, sul - len and chill.
me! if I knew—The night is so dark, and the pass-ers are few."
one tangled gleam That sifts thro' the lil - ies, and wastes on the stream."

p

Rit.

* The chorus should begin while the solo voice is still holding this last note.

The Wayside Cross.—Concluded.

CHORUS.

Near—near thee, my son, is the old way - side cross,

Like a gray fri - ar cowled, in li - chens and moss;

And its cross-beam will point to the bright gold - en span,

That bridg - es the wa - ters so safe - ly for man.

CODA. *pp To be sung after last stanza.*

That bridg - es the wa - ters so safe - ly for man

No. 57.   Jesus Shall Reign.

Watts.

Karl Wilhelm. Arr.

1. Je - sus shall reign wher - e'er the sun Does His suc - cess - ive
2. To Him shall end - less pray'r be made, And end - less prais - es

jour - neys run: His king - dom spread from shore to shore, Till
crown His head: His name, like sweet per - fume, shall rise With

CHORUS.

moons shall wax and wane no more. From north to south the princ - es meet
ev - 'ry morning sac - ri - fice. Peo - ple and realms of ev - 'ry tongue

To pay their hom - age at His feet; While west - ern em - pires
Dwell on His love with sweetest song, And in - fant voic - es

own their Lord, And sav - age tribes at - tend His word.
shall pro - claim Their ear - ly bless - ings on His name.

No. 58. **Prepare Ye the Way.**

P. B.   P. Bilhorn.

1. The voice of Him that cri - eth in the wil - der - ness, Pre-
2. Make straight the highway in the des - ert for our God, Pre-
3. He's com - ing soon to call His ran-som'd chil - dren home, Pre-
4. My broth - er, are you read - y? are you in the light? Pre-

pare ye the way of the Lord; Be - hold the Lord is
pare ye the way of the Lord; Be - hold the gar - ments
pare ye the way of the Lord; Be - hold the day of
pare ye the way of the Lord; Be - hold! He quick - ly

FINE.

com-ing in His right-eous - ness, Pre-pare ye the way of the Lord.
of His Son are dipped in blood, Pre-pare ye the way of the Lord.
vengeance of our Lord will come, Pre-pare ye the way of the Lord.
com - eth, trim your lamps to - night, Pre-pare ye the way of the Lord.

REFRAIN.   D. S.

Prepare ye the way, Prepare ye the way, Prepare ye the way of the Lord;

No. 59. Onward and Upward.

Allegretto moderato.

Dr. H. R. Palmer.

1. On-ward and up-ward and for-ward to-day, On-ward re-
2. On-ward and up-ward and home-ward the while, Up-ward, thy
3. On-ward and up-ward, be strong in the Lord, He is thy

Cres.

new-ing thy strength in the way; Up-ward, tho' rug-ged and
sun-light the Sav-ior's own smile; On-ward, His pres-ence thy
shield, thine e-ter-nal re-ward; He is gone for-ward thy

ff — *Dim.* — *p*

steep be the hill, For-ward the word of the Lord to ful-fill!
shade from the heat, Home-ward, for home aft-er ex-ile is sweet!
place to pre-pare, Home-ward thou go-est to dwell with Him there.

f CHORUS.

On - - ward and up - - - ward with car-ols, with

Onward and upward, on-ward and up-ward with car-ols of

BY PER. H. R. PALMER, OWNER OF COPYRIGHT.

Onward and Upward.—Concluded.

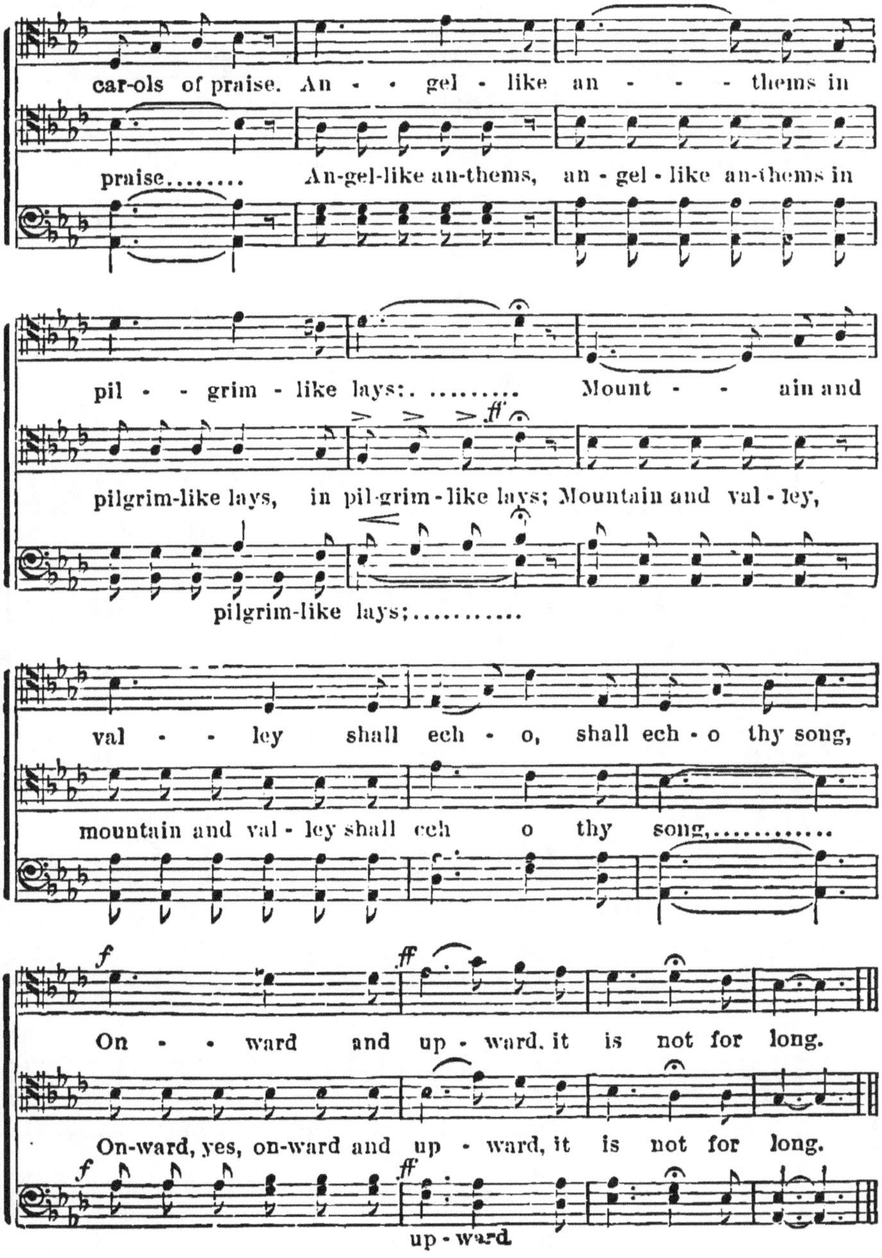

No. 60. Why Not Receive Him?

Ada Blenkhorn.

P. Bilhorn.

1. The Prince of glo - ry left His throne, The sin - ner's friend to be;
2. He feeds the hun - gry soul with bread From life's e - ter - nal tree,
3. He dwells be - fore the great white throne, For need - y souls to pray:

His ho - ly brow with thorns was crown'd, He died on Cal - va - ry:
And bids the thirst - y spir - it drink From liv - ing fount-ains free:
He pleads for those to come to Him, Who did their Lord be - tray:

He suffered thus for thee.
He of - fers this to thee.
He call - eth thee to - day.

CHORUS.

Why not receive Him? Why not believe Him?

While He is call - ing, Call - ing to - day; I will re-ceive Him,

I will believe Him: While He is call-ing, I'll trust in Him to - day.

No. 61.   Drifting Away From God.

Mrs. J. A. Griffith.   P. Bilhorn.

Slowly.   Melody in 2d Tenor.

1. Drift-ing a-way from Christ in thy youth, Drift-ing a-way from
2. Drift-ing a-way from moth-er and home, Drift-ing a-way in
3. Drift-ing a-way on sin's treach'rous tide, Drift-ing where death and
4. Drift-ing a-way from hope's blessed shore, Drift-ing a-way where
5. Why will you drift on bil-lows of shame, spurning His grace a-

mer-cy and truth, Drift-ing to sin in ten-der-est youth,
sor-row to roam, Drift-ing where peace and rest can not come,
dark-ness a-bide, Drift-ing from heav'n a-way in your pride,
wild breakers roar; Drift-ed and strand-ed, wreck'd, ev-er-more,
gain and a-gain? Soon you'll be lost! in sin to re-main,

CHORUS. *Melody in 1st Tenor.*

Drift-ing a-way from God.
Drift-ing a-way from God.
Drift-ing a-way from God.
Far from the light of God.
Ev-er a-way from God.

Broth-er, the Sav-ior has

called you be-fore; See! you are near-ing e-ter-ni-ty's shore!

Rit.

Soon you may perish, be lost ev-er-more, Je-sus now calls for you.

No. 62. Rocked in the Cradle of the Deep.

Emma Willard. J. P. Knight. Arr.

1. Rock'd in the cra-dle of the deep, I lay me
2. And such the trust that still were mine, Tho' storm-y

down in peace to sleep; Se-cure I rest up-on the
winds swept o'er the brine, Or tho' the tem-pest's fier-y

wave. For Thou, O Lord, hast pow'r to save. I know Thou
breath Rous'd me from sleep to wreck and death. In o-cean

wilt not slight my call, For Thou dost mark the spar-row's fall:
cave still safe with Thee, The germ of im-mor-tal-i-ty:

REFRAIN.

And calm and peaceful is my sleep, Rock'd in the cra-dle of the deep,

Rocked in the Cradle of the Deep.—Concluded.

And calm and peaceful is my sleep, Rock'd in the cra-dle of the deep.

No. 63.   Remember Me, O Mighty One!

Anon.   Joanna Kinkel. Arr.

1. When storms around are sweeping, When lone my watch I'm keep-ing,
2. When walk-ing on life's o-cean, Con-trol its rag-ing mo-tion;
3. When weight of sin op-press-es, When dark de-spair dis-tress-es,

'Mid fires of e-vil fall-ing, 'Mid tempters' voic-es call-ing,
When from its dan-gers shrinking, When in its dread deeps sinking,
All thro' the life that's mor-tal, And when I pass death's por-tal,

Chorus.

Remember me, O Might-y One! Re-mem-ber me, O Might-y One!

Home, Sweet Home.

John Howard Payne.

Bishop. Arr.

1. 'Mid pleas - ures and pal - a - ces   though we may roam, Be it
2. An ex - ile from home, splendor daz - zles in   vain— O
3. To us,   in de - spite of the ab - sence of   years How

ev - er   so hum - ble there's   no   place like home!   A
give   me   my low - ly thatch'd cot - tage a - gain; The
sweet—the   re - mem-brance of   home still   ap - pears; From al-

charm from the skies seems to   hal - low us there,   Which
birds sing - ing gai - ly   that come   at   my call,   Give me
lure - ments a - broad which but   flat - ter the   eye,   The un-

REFRAIN.

seek thro' the world   is ne'er met   with else - where.
these and   peace of mind   dear - er than   all.   } Home, home,
sat-is-fied   heart turns and says with a   sigh—

sweet, sweet home! There's no place like   home! There's no place like home!

No. 65. On the Cross.

Words for chorus arr.   P. Bilhorn.

1. A - las! and did my Sav - ior bleed! And did my Sov-'reign die?
2. Was it for crimes that I had done He groan'd up - on the tree?
3. But drops of grief can ne'er re - pay The debt of love I owe:

Would He de - vote that sa - cred head For such a worm as I?
A - maz - ing pit - y! grace unknown! And love be - yond de - gree!
Here, Lord! I give my - self to Thee, 'Tis all that I can do.

CHORUS. *Faster.*

On the cross, on the cross, where I first saw my Lord, And the
burden of my heart roll'd a - way, It was there by faith I re -
ceived His word, And now I am hap - py all the day.

No. 66. The Last Call.

Frank M. Davis.

1. The last call of mer-cy now lin-gers for thee, O sin-ner, re-
2. Oh, slight not the warning now of-fered at last, Till sum-mer is
3. While Je-sus is call-ing, oh, turn not a-way, For swift-ly ap-
4. The last call of mer-cy now lin-gers for thee, Oh, break the strong

ceive it, to Je-sus now flee; He oft-en has called thee, but
end-ed, and har-vest is passed, Till mer-cy, long slight-ed, has
proacheth the dread judgment day, The Spir-it in-vites you, why
fet-ters of sin and be free; The Bride is now call-ing, ye

thou hast re-fused, His of-fered sal-va-tion and love are a-bused.
left thy heart's door, And par-don, sweet par-don are of-fered no more.
will you still roam? Come now to life's wa-ters, ye thirst-y ones, come.
wan-der-ers, come, Ac-cept of sal-va-tion, in heav-en there's room.

CHORUS.

The Spir-it and Bride............... are call-ing for

Spir-it and Bride,

you............ call-ing for you, Oh, haste to the Sav-ior, your days are but

COPYRIGHT, 1893, BY P. BILHORN.

The Last Call.—Concluded.

few, Oh, haste to the Sav - ior, your days are but few.

No. 67. America.

Rev. S. F. Smith. *English Air. Arr.*

1. My coun - try, 'tis of thee, Sweet land of lib - er - ty,
2. My na - tive coun - try, thee, Land of the no - ble free,
3. Let mu - sic swell the breeze, And ring from all the trees,
4. Our fa - ther's God, to Thee, Au - thor of lib - er - ty

Of thee I sing; Land where my fa - thers died, Land of the
Thy name I love; I love thy rocks and rills, Thy woods and
Sweet free - dom's song; Let mor - tal tongues a - wake; Let all that
To Thee we sing: Long may our land be bright With freedom's

pilgrim's pride, From ev - 'ry mount-ain side Let free - dom ring!
tem-pled hills; My heart with rap - ture thrills Like that a - bove.
breathe partake; Let rocks their si - lence break, The sound pro-long.
ho - ly light; Pro - tect us by Thy might, Great God, our King!

No. 68.

He Calleth for Thee.

Ada Blenkhorn. P. Bilhorn.

1. He is call-ing thee, my brother, He is call-ing thee to-day,
2. Now a-rise and say,"My Fa-ther, I have sinn'd and griev'd Thee sore,
3. Ere thou reachest home He'll see thee, and will hast-en thee to greet,
4. He will spread for thee a ban-quet, all the saved will join the throng,

Why from Him in cold and hun-ger wilt thou roam? He so
I have spurned Thy lov-ing fa-vor ma-ny years; Oh, have
With His arms out-stretched to clasp thee to His breast; He will
He will clothe thee in a robe of right-eous-ness; All the

pa-tient-ly en-treat-eth thee no long-er to de-lay,
mer-cy, I be-seech Thee, Thy for-give-ness I im-plore;
glad-ly give thee wel-come and with ten-der-ness will meet;
saints and an-gels, gath-er'd round the throne, will sing the song

For there's food and shel-ter wait-ing thee at home.
With a par-don ban-ish all my doubts and fears."
Thou at home wilt be thy Fa-ther's fa-vored guest.
Of re-demp-tion— and the Fa-ther's name will bless.

He Calleth for Thee.—Concluded.

CHORUS.

He is call - - - ing, He is call - - - ing,
He is call-ing thee, my broth-er, He is call-ing thee to - day,

He is call-ing thee, my broth - er. to come home, (to come home,)

He is call - - - ing, He is call - - - ing,
He is call-ing thee, my broth-er, He is call-ing thee to - day,

He is call-ing thee, my broth - er, to come home. (to come home.)

No. 69.   Wandering Back.

A. M. Hootman.

W. S. Nickle.

1. I am think-ing to-day of the scenes of my youth, And the
2. The old house, crib and barn, are re-placed by a new, And the
3. Yes, I'm glid - ing down the si - lent stream of time, And the

days that have long pass'd and gone;   Of the time when I play'd 'round my
homestead seems strange to me now;   But my tho'ts wander back to my
ev'n-ing of life   is at hand;   And their shadows seem to meet and

dear mother's knee, When she sang me her lul - la - by   song.
dear mother's side, Where in child-hood she oft kissed my brow.
gather at my feet, Like the shells 'mid the bright drifting sand.

Wandering Back.—Concluded.

CHORUS.

No! the days will ne'er re-turn, when I was a boy, The

No! the days will ne'er re-turn, when I was a boy, The

hopes of my youth fade a - way; I am journ'ying a-long to the

hopes of my youth fade a - way; I am journ'ying a-long to the

Rit.   *Repeat pp.*

land of the blest, Where the scenes of my youth ne'er de - cay.

land of the blest, Where the scenes of my youth ne'er de - cay.

No. 70.   Closer to Thee.

The "Lanan."   P. Bilhorn.

1. O Je - sus, my Lord and my Sav - ior, A rock and a
2. Let peace from Thy pres - ence pos - sess me, A peace that a-
3. When close by Thy side I am keep - ing, My path - way is
4. And when my life's jour - ney is end - ing, The waves of the

ref - uge to me; I long to be drawn by Thy fa - vor, Still
bid - ing shall be: And when my temp - ta - tions dis - tress me, O
mark'd out by Thee; And rich are the fields for my reap - ing, While
riv - er I see; Let an - gels from glo - ry de - scend - ing, My

CHORUS.

clos - er and clos - er to Thee.
draw me still clos - er to Thee.
clos - er and clos - er to Thee.
spir - it bear clos - er to Thee.

Clos - er to Thee,

clos - er to Thee, Clos - er, my Lord and my Sav - ior;

Clos - er to Thee, clos - er to Thee, Draw me still clos - er to Thee.

Heaven is My Home.

Adagio e Legato.

1. I'm but a stran - ger here, Heav'n is my home;
2. What tho' the tem - pest rage? Heav'n is my home;
3. Peace! O my troub - led soul, Heav'n is my home;
4. There, at my Sav - ior's side, Heav'n is my home;

Earth is a des - ert drear, Heav'n is my home;
Short is my pil - grim - age, Heav'n is my home;
I soon shall reach the goal; Heav'n is my home;
I shall be glo - ri - fied: Heav'n is my home;

Dan - ger and sor - row stand Round me on ev - 'ry hand;
Time's cold and win - try blast Soon will be o - ver - past;
Swift - ly the race I'll run, Yield up my crown to none;
There are the good and blest, Those I loved most and best,

Heav'n is my Fa - ther - land, Heav'n is my home.
I shall reach home at last; Heav'n is my home.
For - ward! the prize is won; Heav'n is my home.
There, too, I soon shall rest, Heav'n is my home.

No. 72.   Shall I Meet My Sainted Mother?

George Thompson.   *P. Bilhorn.*

1. Shall I meet my saint-ed moth-er, In her home be-yond the skies?
2. When the bells of heav-en ring-ing, Wake the an-gels' song a-gain.
3. All the years of sin and sor-row, That I've suf-fer'd since she died,

Will I see the love-light beaming From her ten-der, lov-ing eyes?
For the wan-der-er re-turn-ing From the paths of sin and pain,
Will be van-ish'd on that mor-row, When I stand by moth-er's side;

Ril.

Will she know me when I meet her, For I'm changed so sad-ly now?
Will my moth-er there be wait-ing, Wait-ing with her look so mild?
Stand with her be-fore the Sav - ior, There among the blood-wash'd throng.

Will she see her fair-haired dar-ling In this old and wrinkled brow?
Will she press me to her bo - som, As she did when but a child?
Join-ing in the heav'nly rap - ture Of the glad re - demp-tion song.

CHORUS.

Yes, I'll meet my saint-ed moth-er, She has gone to mansions fair;

COPYRIGHT, 1886, BY P. BILHORN.

O to meet her, O to greet her, There will be no part-ing there.

No. 73. **The Guiding Star.**

O. E. Murray. A. Beirly.

1. Speak to me, Guid-ing Star, If Thou canst speak so far;
2. Speak to me, Guid-ing Star, Of where my loved ones are;
3. Lord, guide my steps a-right, When my soul takes its flight;
4. O Star of Beth-le-hem, Thou art my soul's bright gem;

Tell of the loved and lost, If safe, or tem-pest-tossed;
I hear the moan-ing sea Sound-ing mys-te-rious-ly;
O Spir-it, pi-lot me O-ver the mys-tic sea,
I know that Thou wilt guide O-ver the dark-some tide;

Tell where my loved ones are, For I soon may cross the bar.
Oh, let Thy light a-far Guide me o'er the o-cean bar.
Be Thou my soul's bright star As I cross the har-bor bar.
Lead me, O Guid-ing Star, As I cross the har-bor bar.

No. 74. **Never to Say Farewell.**

Rev. Elisha A. Hoffman. *Ira Orwig Hoffman.*

1. We jour-ney to the home a-bove, Nev-er to say fare-well,
2. We'll meet our saint-ed par-ents there, Nev-er to say fare-well,
3. We'll meet be-yond life's swell-ing flood, Nev-er to say fare-well,
4. Oh, what a bless-ed hope is this, Nev-er to say fare-well,

To yon fair pal-a-ces of love, Nev-er to say fare-well.
And heav'n with sis-ters, broth-ers share, Nev-er to say fare-well.
Re-deemed and wash'd in Je-sus' blood, Nev-er to say fare-well.
What pure and per-fect hap-pi-ness, Nev-er to say fare-well.

With-in that glo-rious sum-mer-land, The ma-ny jew-eled
Up-on the plains of per-fect light, Up-on the pave-ments
Earth's long, long night will pass a-way, Dis-solv-ing in-to
De-liv-ered from all sin and pain, To reach yon fair, ce-

Rit.

man-sions stand, And there we'll meet, at God's right hand, Never to say farewell.
golden bright, We'll walk with them, enrobed in white, Never to say farewell.
heav'nly day, And we shall with our loved ones stay, Never to say farewell.
les-tial plain, And meet the loved and lost a-gain, Never to say farewell.

Never to Say Farewell.—Concluded.

CHORUS.

Nev-er to say fare - well, Nev-er to say fare - well, Ch,

we shall meet at God's right hand, Nev-er to say fare - well.

No. 75.   The Lord's My Shepherd.

Rouse's Version, 1849.   *Mozart.*

1. The Lord's my Shepherd, I'll not want: He makes me down to lie
2. My soul He doth re - store a - gain; And me to walk doth make
3. Yea, tho' I walk in death's dark vale, Yet will I fear no ill;
4. My ta - ble Thou hast fur - nish-ed In pres-ence of my foes;
5. Good'ness and mer-cy all my life Shall sure-ly fol - low me;

In pas-tures green; He lead-eth me The qui - et wa-ters by.
With-in the paths of right-eous-ness, E'en for His own name's sake.
For Thou art with me; and Thy rod And staff me com-fort still.
My head Thou dost with oil a - noint, And my cup o - ver-flows.
And in God's house for-ev - er-more My dwelling-place shall be.

No. 76. We Walk by Faith.

J. E. Wolfe.　　　　　　　　　　　　　　　　P. Bilhorn.

1. By child-like faith in Christ, the Lord, We have from sin sal-va-tion;
2. How sim-ple is the way of life, 'Tis on-ly to be-lieve Him;
3. Thro' Je-sus' death the debt was paid, Not feel-ing, nor e-mo-tion;
4. We walk by faith and not by sight, How grand is this re-veal-ing!

By ful-ly trust-ing in His word, We pass from con-dem-na-tion.
'Twill end your sor-row and your strife If you will but re-ceive Him.
On Him our sin and guilt was laid; O give Him your de-vo-tion.
'Tis God's own way, and must be right, 'Tis wrong to trust in feel-ing.

Chorus.

We walk by faith and not by sight;

We walk by faith and not by sight; 'Tis God's own way and must be right;

We walk by faith,

We walk by faith and not by sight; We fol-low Christ, the Light.

No. 77.   Prepare to Meet Thy God.

P. B.   P. Bilhorn.

1. Pre - pare to meet thy God, Ere judgment He doth send; E-
2. Pre - pare to meet thy God, He soon may sum-mon thee To
3. Pre - pare to meet thy God, Ere death may call for thee; Pre-
4. Pre - pare to meet thy God, While mer - cy yet is near; For

ter - ni - ty is draw-ing near, The day of grace will end.
come be - fore His judg-ment seat; What will thy an-swer be?
pare, my broth-er, ere you're lost Thro' all e - ter - ni - ty
par - don, look un - to the blood, This warn-ing voice now hear.

CHORUS.

Pre - pare to meet thy God, Pre - pare to meet thy God, The

Rit.

day of grace will soon be gone, Pre - pare to meet thy God.

No. 78. He is Calling You To-day.

P. B.

P. Bilhorn.

1. The Sav - ior hath said That no tears shall be shed
2. Oh! have you not heard Of that won - der - ful word
3. In His word we have read, That His blood hath been shed
4. Yes, the prom - ise is true, That His grace cears us thro'

In the home where He's gone to pre - pare, (pre - pare,)
That bids the poor wan - d'rer to come, (to come,)
For those who have wan - der'd from God, (from God,)
Ev - 'ry tri - al that comes day by day, (by day,)

A man - sion so fair; Yes, my Je - sus is there,
To a feast that is spread, Where we all may be fed;
So re - deem'd from their sin, All may now en - ter in,
If we trust in His word, When the prom - ise is heard;

And He's call - ing for sin - ners to come.
And He's call - ing for sin - ners to come.
While He's call - ing for sin - ners to come.
And He's call - ing for sin - ners to come.

He is Calling You To-day.—Concluded.

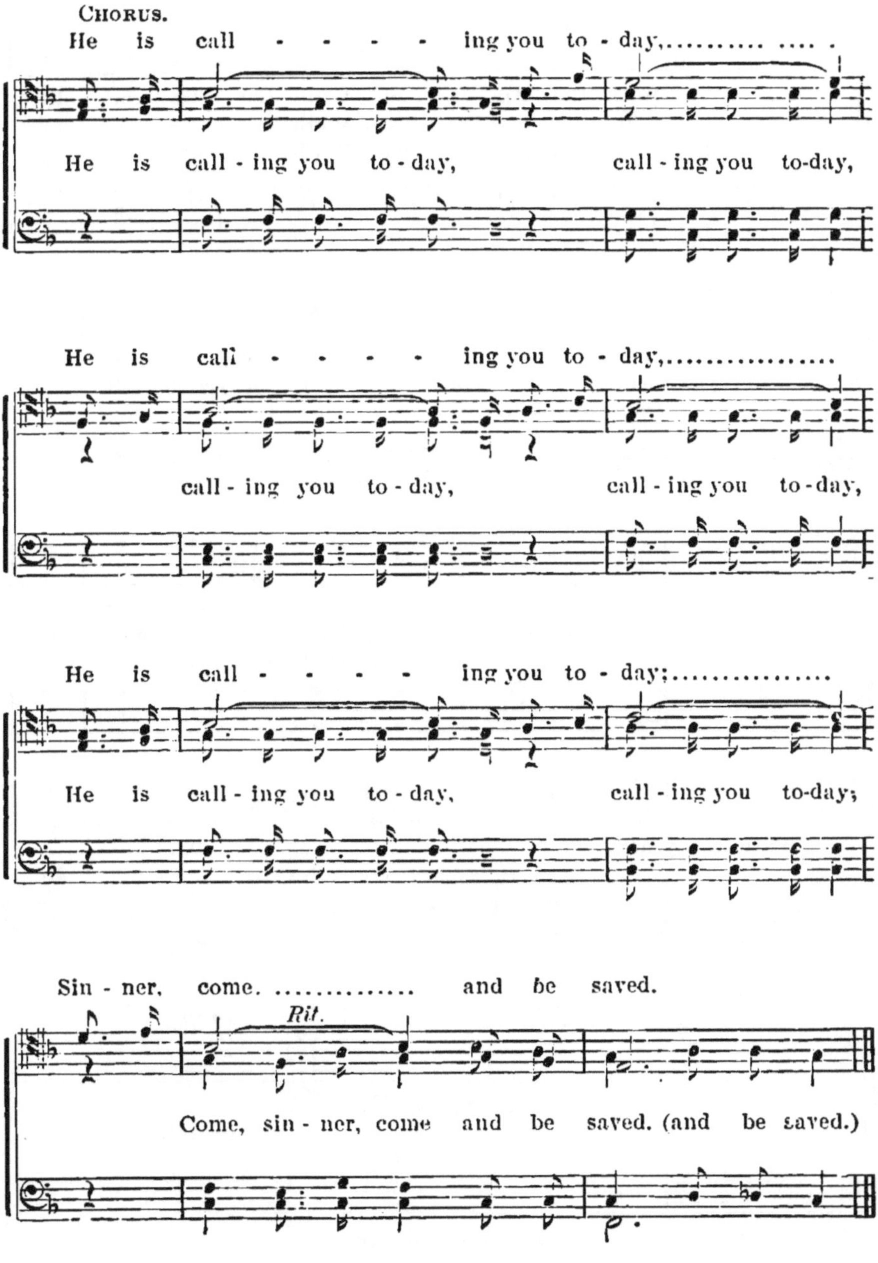

No. 79.

While the Years are Rolling by.

P. B.

E. M. Herndon.

1. There is work that we can do, While the years roll by,
2. List - en to the Mas - ter's call, While the years roll by,
. It may be your joy to win, While the years roll by,

For the la - b'rers are but few, While the years roll by;
Ho! ye reap - ers, one and all, While the years roll by;
Some one from the path of sin, While the years roll by;

Let us work and watch and pray, Till the crown - ing day,
Do not i - dly wait - ing stand, Heed the Lord's com - mand,
To your trust be firm and true, God de - pends on you,

While the years by..........
While the years are roll - ing, roll - ing by

CHORUS.

While the years,........................

Ad lib.

While the years,............
While the years are roll - ing by,

While the Years are Rolling by.—Concluded.

While the years.......... roll by,

While the years roll by,

While the years roll by,

While the years are roll-ing by,

There is work that we can do, While the years are roll-ing by.

No. 80.   **Ye Christian Heralds.**

Bourne H. Draper.   *Zeuner.*

1. Ye Chris - tian her - alds, go, pro - claim Sal -
2. He'll shield you with a wall of fire, With
3. And when our la - bors all are o'er, Then

va - tion thro' Im - man - uel's name; To dis - tant climes
flam - ing zeal your breasts in - spire, Bid rag - ing winds
we shall meet to part no more—Meet with the blood-

the ti - dings bear, And plant the Rose of Shar - on there.
their fu - ry cease, And hush the tem-pest in - to peace.
bought throng to fall, And crown our Je - sus, Lord of all!

No. 81. Bid Him Come in.

P. B.

P. Bilhorn.

1. Oh, what a Sav - ior, He's pleading for you, plead-ing for you,
2. Will you not trust Him as Sav - ior to - day? trust Him to - day?
3. O - pen your heart's door and bid Him come in, bid Him come in,
4. Come now to Je - sus, for why will you die? why will ye die?

pleading for you: Come and ac - cept Him, He's lov - ing and true,
trust Him to - day? He will drive sor-row and sigh - ing a - way,
bid Him come in; He hath redeemed you, He'll cleanse you from sin,
why will you die? While He in mer - cy is com - ing so nigh,

CHORUS.

'Tis Je - sus now plead-ing for you. Shall............ He come
Will you not trust Je - sus to - day?
Oh, bid the dear Sav - ior come in.
Oh, broth - er, then why will you die? Shall He come in?

in?............ Shall.......... He come in?............
Shall He come in? Shall He come in? Shall He come in?

Bid Him Come in.—Concluded.

Repeat pp.

Will.......... you not bid..........the dear Sav - - - ior come in?
He will redeem you and save you from sin, Bid the dear Savior come in.

No. 82.   When I Survey the Wondrous Cross.

German.

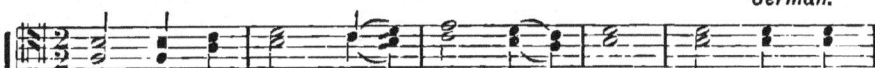

1. When I sur - vey the won - drous cross On which the
2. For - bid it, Lord! that I should boast; Save in the
3. See, from His head, His hands, His feet, Sor - row and
4. Were the whole realm of na - ture mine, That were a

Prince of glo - ry died, My rich - est gain I
death of Christ, my God: All the vain things that
love flow min - gled down; Did e'er such love and
pres - ent far too small; Love so a - maz - ing,

count but loss, And pour con - tempt on all my pride.
charm me most, I sac - ri - fice them to His blood.
sor - row meet, Or thorns com - pose so rich a crown?
so di - vine, De - mands my soul, my life, my all.

Steal Away!

Ethiopian Melody.

Steal a - way, steal a - way, steal a - way to Je - sus!

Steal a-way, steal a-way home, I have not long to stay here.

1. My Lord calls me, He calls me by the thun-der; The
2. Green trees are bend-ing, Poor sin-ners stand trem-bling; The
3. My Lord calls me, He calls me by the light-ning; The

trumpet sounds it in my soul: I have not long to stay here.

I Do Believe.

P. B.

P. Bilhorn.

1. I do be-lieve with all my soul That Je - sus' blood now
2. I do be-lieve with all my heart That Je - sus doth new
3. I do be-lieve that Christ my King Will come a - gain me
4. I do be-lieve in heav'n a - bove There will be naught but

makes me whole! I plunge be-neath the crim - son tide, Which
life im - part! For now I live as ne'er be - fore, In
home to bring! To dwell in man - sions bright and fair, And
pur - est love; And there my ran - somed soul shall sing, Ho-

Rit.   CHORUS.

flowed from out His wound-ed side! ⎫
Christ who liv - eth ev - er - more. ⎪
with Him in His glo - ry share. ⎬ I do be-lieve! I do be-lieve!
san - na to my God and King! ⎭

The cleans-ing blood I now re - ceive: With joy my ran-som'd

Rit.

soul doth sing Ho - san - nas to my God and King.

Take the Step, my Brother.

Mary More.   *J. H. Burke.*

1. Broth-er, at the threshold standing, See you not the o-pen door?
2. See the ban-quet-hall of mer-cy, See thy seat that va-cant stands;
3. Keep thy Lord no long-er wait-ing, He hath died thy soul to win;
4. Just a step—will you not take it, While in pray'r to God we bow?

And the Sav-ior's hand ex-tend-ed, Reaching out to help you o'er?
Think of loved ones wait-ing for thee, See them now with beck'ning hands.
Let His love, thy heart constraining, Lead thee now to en-ter in.
Will you not, your sin for-sak-ing, Trust in Christ and trust Him now?

CHORUS.

Take the step,.............. my breth-er, take it;
Oh, take the step, my broth-er, take it;

Take the step.............. and yield to God;..........
Oh, take the step and yield to God;

Rise! and Christ............ con-fess as Sav · · · · ior;
A-rise! and Christ con-fess as Sav-ior;

Take the Step, my Brother.—Concluded.

Take the step................ and yield to God.
Oh, take the step and yield to God. (and yield to God.)

No. 86. The Savior's Hand.

Peter Bilhorn.
Geo. C. Stebbins.

1. The Sav-ior's hand is knocking, Is knock-ing at thy heart;
2. Hast thou not heard Him knocking, At morn-ing, noon and night?
3. The wound-ed hand of Je-sus, He of-fers now to thee;

O sin-ner, bid Him wel-come, Lest grieved He should de - part.
A-rise, and bid Him en - ter, His pres-ence giv - eth light.
To save, to guide, to keep thee Thro' all e - ter - ni - ty.

CHORUS.

Knock-ing, knock-ing, knock-ing, And long-ing to come in;

Oh! broth-er, bid Him wel-come, He'll cleanse thy heart from sin.

No. 87.   What will Your Harvest be?

Miss Julia H. Johnston.   *P. Bilhorn.*

1. This is the gold-en seed-time, What will the har-vest yield?
2. Sow-ing the seeds of sor-row, Plant-ing the thorns of wrong,
3. What of your seed, be-lov-ed, You who have named His name?
4. Earn-est and faith-ful toil-ers, Bear-ing the pre-cious seed,

What is the seed, O sow-er, Dropped in the wait-ing field?
Look to the end, thou sow-er, Tho' it may tar-ry long;
Is it from out the gar-ner, Pre-cious and still the same?
Sow-ing be-side all wa-ters, Read-y in word and deed,

In-to the o-pen fur-row, Un-der the sun-light free,
Sow-ing in sin and doubt-ing, Seed for e-ter-ni-ty,
Are you a care-less i-dler? What is your hope and plea?
You shall re-turn re-joic-ing, You shall the Mas-ter see;

Seed from your hand is fall-ing, Oh! what will your harvest be?
Reap-ing the fruit here-aft-er, Oh! what will your harvest be?
When you must join the reap-ers, Oh! what will your harvest be?
When the ripe sheaves are garner'd, Oh! blest will your harvest be.

What will Your Harvest be?—Concluded.

CHORUS.   *Rit.*

What will your har-vest be? (har-vest be?) What will your harvest be?
4th v. Blest will your har-vest be, (har-vest be,) Blest will your har-vest be.

No. 88.   Savior, Pilot Me.

J. E. Gould. Arr. by E. M. H.

1. Je - sus, Sav - ior, pi - lot me   O - ver life's tem-pest-uous sea;
2. When th' A-pos-tles' frag-ile bark Struggled with the bil-lows dark,
3. As a moth-er stills her child, Thou canst hush the o - cean wild;
4. When at last I near the shore, And the fear - ful break-ers roar

Unknown waves be-fore me roll, Hid-ing rock and treach'rous shoal:
On the storm-y Gal - i - lee, Thou didst walk a-cross the sea;
Boist'rous waves o - bey Thy will When Thou say'st to them, "Be still."
'Twixt me and the peace-ful rest, Then, while lean-ing on Thy breast

Chart and com - pass came from Thee: Je - sus, Sav - ior, pi - lot me.
And when they be - held Thy form, Safe they glid - ed thro' the storm.
Won-drous Sov-'reign of the sea, Je - sus, Sav - ior, pi - lot me.
May I hear Thee say to me, "Fear not, I will pi - lot thee."

No. 89. Rally Round the Standard.

Ada Blenkhorn.   *P. Bilhorn.*

1. "Arm you for the con - flict!" 'tis the Mas - ter's call,
2. See! the foe ad - vanc - es! num - ber - less they be!
3. For - ward! sol - diers, for - ward! 'tis your Lord's com - mand,
4. Raise your song of tri - umph, spread the joy - ful news,

Hel - met, shield and sword He will pro - vide; Read - y be to fol - low
En - e - mies are they to God and Right: Val - iant sol - diers, fear not!
Strike for God and Heav - en, Truth and Right: On God's strength re - ly - ing,
Join in sing - ing glo - ry to the Son; Glo - ry in the high - est,

where - so - e'er He leads, Standing by our faith - ful Lead - er's side.
God will not for - sake; Do not shrink nor fal - ter at the sight.
vic - t'ry's near at hand, In God's name we'll conquer in the fight.
o Je - ho - vah sing! He, for us, the vic - to - ry has won.

CHORUS.

Ral - ly round the stand - ard, ral - ly round the cross,

Call the faith - ful sol - diers from a - far: Ral - ly round the standard,

Rally Round the Standard.—Concluded.

ff *Rit.*

count-ing all else dross, We shall con-quer in this Ho - ly War.

No. 90. O Glad and Glorious Gospel.

M. Fraser.   James McGranahan.

1. 'Tis a true and faith-ful say - ing, "Je - sus died for sin - ful men;"
2. He has made a full a - tone-ment, Now His sav - ing work is done;
3. Still up - on His hands the nail-prints, And the scars up - on His brow,
4. But re - mem-ber this same Je - sus In the clouds will come a - gain,

Tho' we've told the sto - ry oft - en, We must tell it o'er a - gain.
He has sat - is - fied the Fa - ther, Who ac - cepts us in His Son.
Our Re - deem-er, Lord and Sav - ior, In the glo - ry stand - eth now.
And with Him His blood-bought peo-ple Ev - er - more shall live and reign.

CHORUS.

O glad and glo-rious Gos - pel! With joy we now pro - claim

A full and free sal - va - tion Thro' faith in Je - sus' name.

No. 91.　　　What Time I am Afraid.

Miss J. H. Johnston.　　　　　　　　　　Auld Lang Syne. Arr. by E. M. H.
Melody in 2d Tenor.

1. Sometimes the sky is o-ver-cast, I fear to lose my way;
2. Ac-cus-ing Conscience, like a flame, With-in my spir-it burns,

3. From all the un-known fu-ture days, My tim-id heart re-coils.
4. When twi-light shad-ows soft-ly fall, And night comes on a-pace,

Un-til the storm be o-ver-past, O keep me safe, I pray.
The tempt-er speaks of wrath and shame, My heart, in an-guish, turns

But known to God are all His ways, And all my cares and toils.
In life and death, O Lord of all, I would be-hold Thy face.

In dark-ness, dan-ger, and in doubt, My heart is sore dis-mayed,
To Him whose blood a-tones for me, On whom my heart is stayed,

The wis-dom, pow'r, and might are Thine, But mine the prom-ised aid,
The fi-nal hour, oh! let me meet In peace, and un-dis-mayed,

But "I will trust in Thee, O Lord, What time I am a-fraid."
For "I will trust in Thee, O Lord, What time I am a-fraid."

And "I will trust in Thee, O Lord, What time I am a-fraid."
For "I will trust in Thee, O Lord, What time I am a-fraid."

No. 92.   Jesus, Our Master.

Miss Ada Blenkhorn.   *Arr. by E. M. H.*

Melody in 2d Tenor.

1. Je - sus, our Mas - ter, glad - ly we hear Thy voice Bid - ding us
2. Nar - row the path - way, fal - ter our trembling feet; Oft for Thy
3. Might-y our ar - mor! Sal - va-tion crowns our head, Faith's shining
4. Praise be to Je - sus! praise to our might-y God! Our hal - le-

leave our all and fol-low Thee; We will Thy call o - bey,
prom-ised aid our pray'rs as-cend; Cheered by the an - gel band,
shield is ours where foes as - sail; Our sword, the Word of God,
lu - jahs rise, Sav - ior, to Thee; Our ban-ner's name is love

turn-ing from sin a-way, With Thee, our gracious Lord, ev - er to be.
led by Thy lov-ing hand, Safe shall our journey be un - to the end.
with peace our feet are shod, Clad in our ar - mor bright, we shall prevail
wav-ing our ranks a-bove, Our song is faith, and hope, and vic - to - ry.

No. 93.   Ashamed of Jesus?

Joseph Grigg.   *E. M. Herndon.*

1. Je - sus, and shall............ it ev - er be,...... ....
2. A-shamed of Je - - - - sus! soon-er far..............
3. A-shamed of Je - - - - sus! yes, I may,.............

1. Je - sus, and shall   it ev - er be,

A mor - tal man. .. .. ashamed of Thee?.............
Let ev'n - ing blush............. to own her star;...... .....
When I've no guilt.............. to wash a - way;... ....

A mor - tal man   a-shamed of Thee?

A-shamed of Thee,...... ...... whom an-gels praise,............
He sheds the beams............. of light di - vine.............
No tear to wipe,.............. no good to crave,.............

A-shamed of Thee,   whom an-gels praise,

Whose glo - ries shine through end - less days?...
O'er this be - night - ed soul of mine...
No fear to quell, no soul to save....

Ashamed of Jesus?—Concluded.

Chorus.

A-shamed of Je - - - - sus, that dear Friend............
Ashamed of Je - sus, that dear Friend, that dear Friend,

On whom my hopes..... .... of heav'n de - pend!............
On whom my hopes of heav'n de-pend, heav'n de-pend!

No, when I blush,............. be this my shame,...........
No, when I blush, be this my shame, this my shame,

Rit.

That I no more re - vere His name..................
That I no more re - vere His name, re - vere His name.

No. 94. Christ Hath Arisen.

Julia H. Johnster. P. Bilhorn.

1. Sing, O my soul, re - peat the old - en sto - ry,
2 Spread, spread the news of Je - sus' res - ur - rec - tion,
3. O ris - en Lord, o'er life and death vic - to - rious,
4. He will re - turn? His prom - ise stands re - cord - ed;

Christ on the cross is slain for guilt - y men; Low in the grave, be-
Tell how the stone was quickly rolled a - way; Death could not hold its
Look from Thy throne on all who trust in Thee; By all Thy might, by
Each eye shall see, and ev - 'ry heart shall burn; Still watch and wait, till

hold the Lord of glo - ry, Shout, shout the vic - to - ry! He
King in meek sub - jec - tion, Come, see the emp - ty tomb where
Thine as - cen - sion glo - rious, Thou art ex - alt - ed our Re-
faith and hope re - ward - ed, Sound out the tri - umph-note to

CHORUS.

liv - eth a - gain?
once Je - sus lay.
deem-er to be.
greet His re - turn.

Christ hath a - ris'n! He lives no more to die;

Christic Hath Arisen.—Concluded.

Christ has a-ris'n! He pleads for us on high; Tell of His might, and
praise His Ho-ly name, Oh, let the ransom'd ones His great love proclaim.

While Life Prolongs.

Timothy Dwight, D. D., 1800.   *Dr. L. Mason, 1839.*

1. While life pro-longs its precious light, Mer-cy is found, and peace is given:
2. While God invites, how blest the day! How sweet the Gospel's charming sound!
3. Soon, borne on time's most rapid wing, Shall death command you to the grave;
4. In that lone land of deep de-spair No Sabbath's heav'nly light shall rise,
5. Now God invites; how blest the day! How sweet the Gospel's charming sound!

But soon, ah, soon, approaching night Shall blot out ev'ry hope of heav'n.
Come, sinners, haste, oh, haste away, While yet a pard'ning God is found.
Be-fore His bar your spirits bring, And none be found to hear or save.
No God regard your bit-ter pray'r, No Sav-ior call you to the skies.
Come, sinners, haste, oh, haste away, While yet a pard'ning God is found.

No. 96. Press toward the Mark.

El. Nathan.

James McGranahan.

1. Ring out the word from Christ the Lord, Our Captain in the skies, To
2. He'll give the grace to win the race To him who bravely tries; For
3. Keep, then, the road; fight on for God, Tho' en - e - mies a - rise; The
4. Bear, then, the cross: count all things loss; On Je-sus fix your eyes; Till

all the saved who have believ'd:"Press toward the mark for the prize."
Je - sus' sake the mes-sage take:"Press toward the mark for the prize."
Lord, with thee thy strength shall be:"Press toward the mark for the prize."
Christ has come, till heav'n is won:"Press toward the mark for the prize."

REFRAIN.
Press toward the mark for the prize,

Press toward the mark for the prize,
Press toward the mark for the
Press

Press toward the mark for the prize,
Press toward the mark for the prize, Let us
prize, Press toward the mark for the prize,
toward the mark for the prize,

suffer with Him and the "Well done" win, Press toward the mark for the prize.

Index

INDEX.

ANDERSON BROS., MUSIC TYPOGRAPHERS, 334 DEARBORN ST., CHICAGO, ILL.